EXTRA-SPECIAL BIBLE ADVENTURES
FOR CHILDREN'S MINISTRY

BY
CHRISTINE
YOUNT

Group®

Loveland, Colorado

DEDICATION

To all the children on an exciting journey to know God better, especially Grant and Abigail.

ACKNOWLEDGMENTS

I could never have written this book without the loving support of my husband, Michael. Thanks for being my sounding board and for being excited about this concept. I'm also indebted to my teachers who showed me what a blast it is to know God. Thank you to Carolyn Teague, the most creative woman on earth; to Max Barnett, a man who knows God personally; to Harold Bullock, a pastor whose faith goes far beyond church walls; and to Thom and Joani Schultz, two people with an insatiable appetite for effective teaching methods. This book is your book in me!

Extra-Special Bible Adventures for Children's Ministry
Copyright © 1994 Christine Yount

Unless otherwise noted, Scripture quoted from The Youth Bible, New Century Version, copyright © 1991 by Word Publishing, Dallas, Texas 75039. Used by permission.

Credits
Edited by Jennifer Root Wilger
Cover designed by Liz Howe
Cover illustration by Paula Becker
Interior designed by Jean Bruns
Illustrations by Jan Knudson and Bonnie Matthews

Library of Congress Cataloging-in-Publication Data
Yount, Christine.
    Extra-special Bible adventures for children's ministry / by Christine Yount.
        p.   cm.
    ISBN 1-55945-257-9
    1. Christian education of children. 2. Experiental learning.
I. Title.
BV1475.2.Y68 1994
268'.432—dc20   94-28191
10 9 8 7 6 5 4 3 2   03 02 01 00 99 98 97 96 95   CIP
Printed in the United States of America.

TABLE OF
CONTENTS

HOW TO USE THIS BOOK

Welcome to the journey of a lifetime! With *Extra-Special Bible Adventures for Children's Ministry,* you'll guide the children in your upper-elementary ministry on a multisensory journey through the Bible. Kids will discover what it was like for Adam and Eve to live in paradise and to then lose it. They'll flee from Egypt and wander in the wilderness with the Israelites. They'll feel the heat Daniel's friends felt when they defied the king and obeyed God. They'll journey with Jesus and Paul and learn firsthand what it means to follow Christ.

Use the journeys to spice up your regular Sunday school time. Or use them in midweek, after-school, or vacation Bible school programs to keep kids coming back for more. After these journeys, your kids will never look at the Bible as a boring textbook; they'll begin to see the Bible for what it is—a record of the faith journeys of God's people long ago and a guidebook for their journey of faith today.

So dig in! The journeys teach kids important Bible lessons through active and interactive learning experiences. You can find more information about how these exciting learning structures will enhance your journeys on pages 6-7. Your kids will love the fun and adventure that active and interactive learning provide.

And you can relax and enjoy the journey. With active and interactive learning, you don't have to have all the answers—you just need to be adventurous and willing to risk and learn alongside your students. Ask God to be your teacher each week. You'll be pleasantly surprised at all you'll learn as you're open to the Holy Spirit's teaching.

CHOOSING A JOURNEY

Where should you start? That's up to you and your group. Each journey can stand alone, so you can start with any of the five journeys—as long as you complete each journey from start to finish before embarking on another one.

Each journey comes complete with

● **tour-guide tips**—background information you'll need to guide kids on the journey;

● **scenery pointers**—ideas to help you turn your room into a desert, village, or other destination;

● **destination**—clear objectives for what kids will accomplish;

● **gear**—a detailed list of everything you'll need for the journey;

● **packing tips**—preparations you'll need to make before the journey; and

● **road signs**—helpful hints to let you

know what you can expect along the way.

Each destination includes two objectives. The first objective focuses on a characteristic of God. Kids will learn that God is creative, holy, and faithful. They'll discover that God wants us to obey him and that God sent Jesus to die for our sins. The second objective helps kids develop Christlike character qualities. Kids will learn kindness, teamwork, love, and determination. As you choose your first journey, think about your kids' needs and choose a journey that will meet those needs. Remember—there's no right or wrong order!

PLANNING FOR THE JOURNEYS

As with any journey, preparation ensures success. Before kids arrive...

● Review the journey several times so you can enjoy it with your kids. You'll all have more fun if you're not tied to the pages of this book. Briefly outline the jour-ney on a 3×5 card to help you remember what comes next.

● Familiarize yourself with the Scripture passages used in the journey. Choose a Bible translation that kids will understand.

● Collect all the supplies you'll need for the journey. If it's difficult for you to collect supplies, enlist the help of an adult sponsor. Divide up the supply list and share the load.

● Follow the scenery pointers to create the environment for your journey. And add to them. The exciting classroom environment you create will stimulate learning and help kids imagine they're really on a journey.

● Remember refreshments. Some journeys include snack ideas related to the theme, but kids always appreciate any food you bring!

● Remind yourself why you've chosen this journey for your kids. Imagine the impact it will have on their lives. Pray for a meaningful, growth-filled time together.

THE LEARNING ADVENTURE

UNDERSTANDING ACTIVE AND INTERACTIVE LEARNING

With active learning, kids learn by doing. Instead of sitting passively and absorbing information from the teacher, kids involve all their senses in activities that enable them to discover Bible truths for themselves. The teacher leads kids through an experience and then helps them talk about what just happened, relate it to the Bible, and apply it to their lives.

Interactive learning employs the principles of active learning and adds yet another dimension—group activities. But with interactive learning, group activities are much more than just kids working or playing together. Kids learn important social skills that transfer into Christian character. The journeys in *Extra-Special Bible Adventures for Children's Ministry* are set up to enhance opportunities for such growth to occur.

When kids engage in competitive activities, they learn to succeed at others' expense. When kids engage in interactive activities, they learn to benefit from each other's successes. Each student must contribute if the group is to succeed, so kids learn to help and encourage each other.

Interactive learning sets up the teacher as a facilitator rather than the sole source of information. Kids have to rely on each other. As a result, kids can use their strengths in certain areas to help others who are weaker in those areas. Skilled readers can help beginning readers, athletes can help nonathletes, artists can help nonartists—the list goes on and on!

USING ACTIVE AND INTERACTIVE LEARNING

Because active and interactive learning focus kids' attention on the task and on each other, you'll need a signal to let them know when it's time to stop what they're doing and look to you for their next directions. Consider using a fun noisemaker that fits your journey, such as a ram's horn or a tambourine. Or simply flash the lights or raise your hand. Whatever signal you use, you'll find it provides welcome relief from repeating, "May I have your attention, please?" over and over.

Be sure you inform kids ahead of time about your signal. You may even want to involve your kids in choosing the signal— and the response they'll give when they see or hear it. You might agree that they'll raise their hands when you raise your hand, or

clap when you sound a horn. After you give the signal, don't begin or continue talking until everyone has given the agreed-upon response. Unless kids let you know they're tired of it, you may want to use the same signal during all the journeys.

Each journey in *Extra-Special Bible Adventures for Children's Ministry* uses one or more of the following interactive-learning structures. Each time a learning structure is used, the corresponding symbol will appear beside it. You can refer to this guide any time you need more information about a particular learning structure. You can also use this guide for future reference when you want to incorporate interactive learning into other class sessions when you're finished with this book.

PAIR SHARE

Students turn to a partner and share ideas or opinions or respond to a question or problem presented by the leader. You can also have kids write their answers, then pair them up with kids who have the same or different opinions.

CORNERS

Ask a question with four answers and then designate a different corner for each answer. Have kids write down their answers and go to the corresponding corner. Kids in each corner can then discuss why they gave the answer they did.

LINEUPS

Create a masking tape or imaginary line on the floor. Designate answer areas for each end of the tape, such as "yes/no" or "agree/disagree." Ask a question or read a statement and have kids line up on the tape

to indicate whether or not they agree. Students who aren't sure will stand in the middle of the tape. Students who strongly agree or disagree will stand at opposite ends of the tape. You can then pair up kids with similar or different opinions for discussion.

LEARNING GROUP

Kids form small groups to work on an issue or a project. For example, they may do an investigative Bible study or figure out how to construct a biblical craft. This learning structure capitalizes on group members' problem-solving abilities.

Each person in the learning group may be assigned a specific role. When kids each have a specific responsibility, they're more likely to contribute to the group's activities, resulting in more learning for everyone. The following roles may be used in this book:

● **Encourager**—Praises individual and team efforts.

● **Gatekeeper**—Makes sure everyone participates fully.

● **Timekeeper**—Makes sure the group is accomplishing its goals on time.

● **Recorder**—Writes down answers agreed on by the group. He or she also makes notes of key thoughts expressed during group discussion.

● **Reader**—Reads Bible passages aloud as other group members follow along.

● **Reporter**—Reports the group's answers to the class.

You can use role assignments to enhance any group activity. The roles listed above will work with most activities. You may want to make up additional roles for ▼

specific activities. For example, when kids decorate the room for a party in the Genesis journey, you could assign kids to be balloon inflaters, streamer hangers, or confetti tossers.

ROUND TABLE

All group members contribute ideas to one sheet of paper. When you give the signal, kids each write or draw their answers, then pass the paper on. This learning structure also works with multiple sheets of paper. Each group member could have a sheet of paper that is passed around.

ROUND ROBIN

This is a verbal version of Round Table. On the signal, kids take turns giving their answers orally.

JIGSAW

Form groups and have group members number off from one to four. Then designate a number for each corner of the room. Have all the ones go to corner #1, all the twos to corner #2, and so on. Have kids work in their corners to learn part of the content you'll be covering. On the signal, have kids return to their original groups and teach other group members what they learned in their corners.

ASSEMBLY LINE

Have students line up side by side to work on a project. Each student works on one component of a project and then passes the project down the line until it's completed. The completed project depends on each child's contribution.

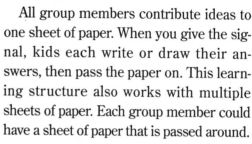

BUILDING CHRISTIAN CHARACTER WITH INTERACTIVE LEARNING

Biblical concepts and Christlike character qualities are built into the activities in each journey. Knowing the qualities kids will learn in each journey will help your class succeed with interactive learning. Introduce the Christlike character quality at the beginning of the journey and then define, reinforce, and evaluate the quality all along the way.

Each journey in *Extra-Special Bible Adventures for Children's Ministry* focuses on one or more of the following character qualities:

● **Teamwork**—Working together with others to achieve a goal.

● **Kindness**—Treating others with respect and gentleness.

● **Determination**—Doing everything possible to reach a goal.

● **Love**—Actively pursuing the best interests of others.

● **Encouragement**—Supporting others and helping them to have confidence.

How do you teach Christlike character qualities? Work on one quality at a time. For example, if you're starting with love, begin by explaining what love is and why it's important. Talk with kids about what they can expect to see and hear as they begin to put their love into practice.

Use a cross chart like the one in the next column to help kids identify love at work in the classroom. Draw a large cross on a sheet of newsprint. Write "love" (or the quality you'll be teaching) at the top of the chart. On the left side of the cross, write "Sounds like." On the right side of the cross, write "Looks like." Ask

kids to help you fill in each side of the cross chart, one side at a time.

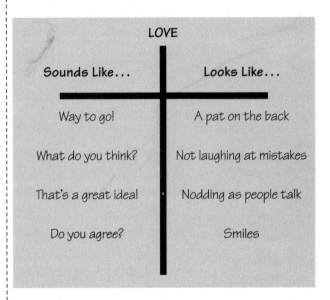

Once you've completed your cross chart together, you're ready to embark on your journey. Model character qualities throughout the journey and praise examples of character qualities you notice during class. Monitor groups to look for Christlike character qualities in action. Let kids know you'll be traveling around the room, eavesdropping on their interactions and looking for that lesson's character quality. Each week, photocopy the "Christlike Character-Quality Observation Chart" (p. 9) to record your observations.

At the end of class, share your observations with students. Affirm individuals and groups who used the character quality by giving them one of the "Christlike-Character Awards" (pp. 11-13). In addition to your feedback, kids will enjoy and benefit from evaluating each other. Every now and then, have groups evaluate themselves using the "How's It Going?" evaluation form (p. 10).

CHRISTLIKE CHARACTER-QUALITY OBSERVATION CHART

DATE	QUALITY	JOURNEY

Record your observations about ways kids put today's character quality into action. Your observations might look like the italicized examples below. At the end of class, share your observations with students.

GROUP	STUDENT	COMMENTS
2	*Kayla*	*Helped each other design poster.* *Asked other group members not to make fun of Jeremy.*

How's It Going?

How's your group getting along? Work together to fill out the evaluation below and then talk about ways you could work together even better.

1.

We each contributed ideas:

___often

___sometimes

___never

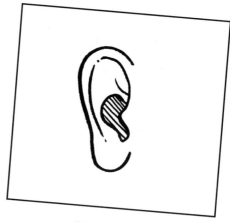

2.

We listened to each other:

___often

___sometimes

___never

3.

We encouraged each other:

___often

___sometimes

___never

4.

We built on each other's ideas:

___often

___sometimes

___never

CHRISTLIKE-CHARACTER AWARDS

When you see groups or individuals working together and showing the character quality you're learning, give them one of the following Christlike-character awards.

Copyright © Christine Yount. Published in *Extra-Special Bible Adventures for Children's Ministry* by Group Publishing, Inc., Box 481, Loveland, CO 80539.

CHRISTLIKE-CHARACTER AWARDS
continued

DETERMINATION AWARD

Our class applauds your efforts!

CLAP! CLAP!

Signed: _____

Date: _____

KINDNESS AWARD

Your kindness is one of a kind!

#1

Signed: _____

Date: _____

CHRISTLIKE-CHARACTER AWARDS

continued

Journey Through GENESIS

*"The earth belongs to the Lord, and everything in it—
the world and all its people."*
PSALM 24:1

What a glorious world God made! Trees, plants, and flowers cover the earth. Thousands of creatures roam its surface—the tiny ladybug, the thundering elephant, and everything in between. Everywhere we look we see all kinds of plants and animals and all kinds of people—no two exactly alike. Our world reflects the immense creativity of the One who made it. But that creativity is most evident in people, God's last and greatest creation. Only people were created in God's image, to think and reason, to feel emotions, and to love and worship God.

Nothing could have been more perfect—until sin entered the world. Instead of following God's directions, Adam and Eve chose to go their own way. As a result, they had to leave the beautiful garden home God had given them. God's world remains a beautiful place, but its beauty is now marred by the presence of sin. Since Adam and Eve, generation after generation of people have continued to ignore and disobey God.

This three-week journey leads kids through Genesis 1–3. They'll fill the classroom with images from God's creation as they express their God-given creativity. They'll enjoy games, music, food—all the things kids love best—as they party in the garden paradise they've created. Then they'll discover how sin spoiled a perfect world as they're forced to tear down their elaborate creations.

Most of your students understand that their actions have consequences. If they break a window playing baseball, they'll have to pay for it. If they don't study for a test, they'll get a poor grade. This journey will help kids learn that sin has consequences, too. Kids will learn how sin entered the world and understand why our sins can't go unpunished. They'll also learn that Jesus died for our sins so we can one day re-enter paradise.

You don't need to create any special classroom environment for this journey. Kids will create their own garden paradise in the first week of this journey. You may want to bring in a recording of jungle sounds or music for kids to listen to as they work. You can obtain sound effects recordings at your local public library.

WELCOME TO PARADISE

GENESIS 1

● Kids will learn that God is creative.
● Kids will learn determination.

You'll need Bibles; photocopies of the "Christlike Character-Quality Observation Chart" (p. 9); and art supplies such as newspapers, newsprint, markers, scissors, string, colored construction paper, poster board, tempera paint, paintbrushes, glue, and tape. If you have a cassette tape of jungle sounds, you'll need a cassette player.

Kids will also enjoy any additional art supplies you can provide. Extras could include colored cellophane, tissue paper, stuffing or batting, glitter, sequins, feathers, felt, fabric scraps, glow-in-the-dark paint, or modeling clay.

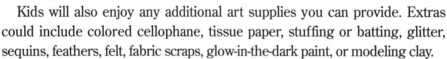

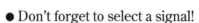

● Don't forget to select a signal!
● Before class, get permission to leave kids' creations in place for the next two weeks. It's essential for this journey that you let the custodian, your director, and any other teachers know not to disturb your room decor.
● You'll also need to select and be prepared to lead two or three familiar praise songs.

THE JOURNEY: Day 1

PREPARE WITH PRAYER

(up to 5 minutes)

Say: **Today marks the start of an exciting adventure for our class. We're going to be learning about events that happened long ago in Bible times. But we're not just going to read or talk about them; we're going to create a Bible-times environment right here in our classroom and experience Bible events as if we were actually there. It will be like taking a journey back to Bible times.**

Ask:

● **When have you taken a journey?** (When I went to my grandma's for Thanksgiving; when our family went on vacation; when my scout troop went camping.)

● **What was your favorite part of the journey?** (Flying in an airplane; coming home to my friends; seeing my cousins.)

● **What new things did you discover on the journey?** (I learned how to put up a tent; I saw a bald eagle; I went to three states I'd never been to before.)

Say: **Journeys are a lot of fun. We get to be with our family or friends, and we get to do fun things and see new places. Sometimes we learn new things when we go on journeys. During our journey back to Bible times, we'll be learning new things about God and about each other. We'll have to work together and help each other along the way. Let's ask God to help us do that.**

Pray: **Dear God, thanks for giving us the Bible to help us learn about you.**
Please be with us as we go on our journey. Help us work together as we learn new things. In Jesus' name, amen.

DESTINATION: DETERMINATION

(up to 5 minutes)

Say: **Our Bible journey is going to take us back to the time of Creation. We'll learn how God created everything and discover what it might've been like to live in a brand-new world. As we work together, we'll also be learning determination. What do you know about determination?** (Let kids respond.)

Say: **Determination means you've really set your mind on doing something, and you're going to do whatever it takes to get that thing done. Jesus was determined to show us God's love. He talked to people, fed them, healed them—all to show them that God loved them.**

We can show determination just like Jesus did. If you're really tired at the end of a hike, but you keep walking because you want to make it to the end, that's determination. If you want to do better in spelling, and you study your spelling words at home every night until you get them all right, that's determination.

Ask:

● **What other examples of determination can you think of?** (I keep practicing my piano piece until I can play it without making a mistake; I played catch with my dad every day last spring so I could make the school baseball team.)

● **Why is determination important?** (It keeps you from giving up; if you're working together, it makes you help each other so you can get the job done.)

Say: **As we go on our journey together, be thinking of ways you can show determination. To help us remember about determination, let's make a chart.**

Post a sheet of newsprint and draw a cross chart as described on page 8. Write "determination" above the cross.

Say: **On the left side of this cross, let's write what determination sounds like. What kinds of things would you hear people say if they're showing determination?**

List kids' responses on the newsprint. They may say that determination sounds like "We're almost done; we only have five minutes" or "We're almost there—keep going. We can make it."

Say: **On the right side of the cross, let's write what determination looks like. What kinds of things would you see people doing if they're showing determination?**

List kids' responses on the newsprint. They may say that determination looks like everyone working hard to finish a project or people offering to help each other so they can get a project done on time.

Say: **As we go on our journey, you can use this chart to help you remember to practice determination. I'll be looking at our chart, too and watching for people or groups who are showing determination.**

CREATIVITY EXPRESS
(up to 40 minutes)

Form six groups and assign each group one of the following days of Creation from Genesis 1. Each group should have two or more people and an equal mix of older and younger kids. If you have fewer than 12 kids, assign some groups more than one day.

p. 7

● The first day (Genesis 1:1-5)
● The second day (Genesis 1:6-8)
● The third day (Genesis 1:9-13)
● The fourth day (Genesis 1:14-19)
● The fifth day (Genesis 1:20-23)
● The sixth day (Genesis 1:24-31)

Distribute Bibles and set out the art supplies you've brought. Say: **Read your Bible passage and then use the art supplies to create the part of Creation your passage talks about. Think about all the different kinds of water, clouds, plants, and animals God made. You can draw pictures, make paper sculptures—you use the supplies any way you want as you design your part of Creation. You'll have 30 minutes to fill the classroom with Creation. I'll give this signal** (demonstrate the signal you've chosen) **to let you know that time is up and that we're ready to move on to something else.**

Circulate between groups to help kids get started on their creations. Encourage kids to work together to come up with creative ideas and to share the work of carrying them out. You may need to help groups divide up the work so chil-

Use this list as a quick reference to help you know what elements of Creation each group is working on.

● Day 1: light, day, and night
● Day 2: air and sky
● Day 3: land, seas, and plants
● Day 4: sun, moon, and stars
● Day 5: sea animals and birds
● Day 6: animals, Adam and Eve

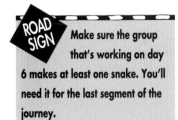
ROAD SIGN Make sure the group that's working on day 6 makes at least one snake. You'll need it for the last segment of the journey.

dren of all ages are involved in age-appropriate ways.

If you have a recording of jungle sounds or music, play it in the background as kids work. If groups finish early, have them help other groups. If groups are having trouble thinking of ideas, suggest one from the following list:

● Hang glittery stars on strings from the ceiling.

● Borrow lamps from another area of the church (if your room doesn't have any) to use as the sun and the moon.

● Use poster board and markers or paints to make trees or flowers and tape them to the wall.

● Hang birds from the ceiling and

tape fish to the baseboards of your room.

● Draw and cut out animals from poster board.

● Make 3-D creatures by drawing animals or fish on two layers of construction paper or newsprint. Cut out the creatures and then staple them together on three sides. Stuff them with newspaper and staple the last side.

● Make an ocean on one wall.

● Make construction paper leaves. Have a boy and a girl place the leaves in their hair and stand as statues to represent Adam and Eve.

After kids finish their creations or the 30 minutes are up, gather chil-

ROAD SIGN As kids focus on the goal of completing their project, affirm them for their determination. You may say something such as "Wow! This group is really determined to get the job done!" or "Jamie, I admire your determination." Use the "Christlike Character-Quality Observation Chart" (p. 9) to record your observations.

PAIR SHARE

p. 6

dren together. Have groups each read their passages and point out their contributions to the "world" you've created in your classroom. After each group has shown its creation, applaud their contribution and say together, "And it was good."

After the last group has shared, say: **You really put a lot of work into your creations. They look great! Now I'd like you to find a partner from another group and get ready to talk about what it was like to create all those creatures and clouds and suns and stars.**

Wait for students to find partners, then ask the following questions, one at a time. Pause after you ask each question to allow time for pairs to discuss it.

● **How did you feel as you made your part of creation?** (Great, it was fun to make something out of all those supplies; frustrated because my group wouldn't let me help; it was hard to make all the animals in half an hour.)

● **How do you think God felt when he created the world?** (Good; happy; excited; tired when he was done.)

● **God showed a lot of creativity when he made the world. How does your partner's creation show creativity?** (She thought of using sequins for fish scales; the lion he drew looks so real; her group brought in real leaves for their trees.)

● **How do you show creativity at home or school?** (By playing the guitar; by writing stories; by doing projects with my mom.)

Give the signal and wait for kids' attention. Say: **The creations you made today show lots of creativity. We're all pretty creative, but God is even more**

creative! **He made the entire world out of nothing. He thought of all the different kinds of animals and where they would live and what they would eat. He made people with legs for walking, hands for picking things up, lungs for breathing, and minds for thinking and creating. God made us in his image, and that means we're creative, too. We can't make something out of nothing like God can, but we can take the things God's given us and make them into beautiful creations as you've done today.**

Being creative is more than being artistic. Every time you figure out a new way to wear your hair or a different way to win a video game, that's God's creativity at work in you. Creativity is using your determination to create something new—in the same way that God did.

THE SEVENTH DAY
(up to 10 minutes)

Gather children in the center of the room and have them sit down. Ask a volunteer to read aloud Genesis 2:2-3. Have other kids follow along in their Bibles.

Say: **After God created the world, he rested. Let's rest now and thank God for all he has made.**

Lead children in thanking God for creation. As you name each element of creation, have the children who made that part of creation go to it, touch it, and say together, "We thank you, God." For example, say, "For your unique fish that swim in the seas," and then wait for kids to move to the fish and say, "We thank you, God." Encourage the rest of the kids to silently thank God for those things, too.

Use this prayer as a guide:

God, you are a creative God. You made the world and all that is in it. You made us in your image to be creative as you are creative. We thank you, God.

For the light you've given us to make day and night... (Pause for children to respond.)

For the sky you've placed above our heads... (Pause for children to respond.)

For the land we live on and the seas we explore. For the plants you've given to nourish us... (Pause for children to respond.)

For the sun that warms our days and the moon and stars that light our nights... (Pause for children to respond.)

For the unique fish you've placed in the sea and the birds that greet us on a cool, spring day... (Pause for children to respond.)

For the animals you've given us and for making us in your image... (Pause for children to respond.)

Thank you, God, for all you've made. In Jesus' name, amen.

After your prayer of thanks, lead children in singing two or three familiar praise songs.

Say: **Your creations are so wonderful that we're going to leave them up for our whole journey. You've transformed our classroom into a brand-new world. Next week we'll have fun together as we see what it was like for Adam and Eve to live in God's new world. Let's close by giving God a big cheer for all the great things he's made.**

Have children hold hands in a circle and on the count of three, yell, "Yea, God!"

Before they leave, give groups their "Christlike Character-Quality Observation Charts" and have them discuss ways they can improve their determination next week. Encourage kids to come next week when you'll celebrate the great world God created.

PARADISE PARTY

GENESIS 2:4-23

- Kids will learn that God deserves our praise.
- Kids will learn determination.

You'll need Bibles, paper crowns, noisemakers, confetti, streamers, balloons, contemporary Christian music cassettes or CDs, a cassette or CD player, two apples, two eyedroppers, two same-size cups, a bucket of water, fruit punch, fresh fruit kabobs, cut-up vegetables with dip, and masking tape.

You'll need to be prepared to lead kids in an upbeat praise song, such as "How Majestic Is Your Name" or "We Bow Down," available in *Group's Praise and Worship Songbook* (Group Publishing).

THE JOURNEY: Day 2

PARTY PRAISE

(up to 15 minutes)

As kids arrive, give them noise-makers, confetti, streamers, and balloons. Say: **Today we're going to celebrate the great world God created. We'll have a party to enjoy the mini "paradise" you've set up. Use the supplies I've given you to create a party atmosphere in our garden, then we'll all celebrate and have fun together.**

Help kids use the party decorations to decorate the room. As they work, play kids' favorite contemporary Christian music on a CD or cassette player. Encourage kids to have fun as they help each other decorate.

After about 10 minutes, turn down the music and give the signal to let kids know they need to finish up their decorations. Say: **Wow! This place looks great! You're all creative decorators. It's great to be able to enjoy God's creation together. Let's start our party by praising God for all he's made.**

Distribute Bibles and have kids look up Psalm 8. When everyone has found the passage, ask several volunteers to read it. Have each volunteer read two or three verses. Ask:

ROAD SIGN As kids put up the decorations, watch for examples of determination. You may see kids lifting each other up to reach the ceiling or forming an assembly line to blow up, tie, and hang balloons. Praise examples of determination that you notice.

ROAD SIGN Kids will enjoy music from recordings such as *A Cappella Kids,* from Maranatha! Music or *Hallelujah Hop* from Brentwood Music. If you're not sure what your students will like, ask one or two of them to bring in Christian tapes or CDs from home.

● **How do you feel knowing that God put people in charge of everything he made?** (Special; honored; not sure what that means.)

● **What's one way God has shown his love and care for you lately?** (Answered my prayers; helped me do my best; through my family.)

Say: **God loves and cares for each one of us. He deserves our thanks and praise, today and every day, for all the great things he does for us. We're going to sing a song to praise him now, and as we sing, I'll put a crown on everyone's head. You can wear your crown as a party hat and as a reminder that God created us to be in charge of creation.**

Lead kids in singing an upbeat praise song. As they sing, put paper crowns on their heads. Then say: **Our God is a great God, and he cares about us. Now that's something to celebrate. Let the party begin!**

PARADISE PLAY

(up to 25 minutes)

Lead kids in several of the following games to help them enjoy paradise.

ROAD SIGN If the weather's nice, you might want to play one or more of these games outside. If you play inside, have kids shuffle instead of running in Animal Tag. Be sure to lay down plastic if you play Come to the River indoors.

● **Animal Tag**

Choose one student to be "It." Have It try to tag the other kids. If a child calls out an animal name before he or she is tagged, that child is safe. However, each animal name may be used only once. If an animal name is called out twice, that child isn't safe and can be tagged. When a child is tagged, he or she becomes It and play continues.

● **Apple Relay**

Form two lines. Give the first person in each line an apple to hold under his or her chin. When you give the signal, have kids pass the apples down the line. They must each hold the apple under their chins until the next person in line takes it and holds it under his or her chin. Kids may not use their hands to pass the apples, except to pick them up and put them back under their chins if they fall to the floor. Continue until the first apple reaches the end of the line, then declare a winner.

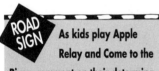

ROAD SIGN

As kids play Apple Relay and Come to the River, comment on their determination to do well as a team. You may notice more examples of determination on "losing" teams as they try again and again to pass their apples or fill their buckets.

● **Come to the River**

Form two teams. Give each team an eyedropper and a paper cup marked with a fill line about halfway up the cup. Place a bucket of water at one end of the room. Have teams line up at the other end of the room. When you give the signal, the first teammates in line must run to the bucket and fill up their eyedroppers, return to their teams, and squirt the water in their cups. The next teammate in line must take the eyedropper and repeat the process. The first team to fill its cup to the fill line wins.

If you have time and kids are interested, encourage them to think up other games they might have enjoyed in paradise. After about 25 minutes, give the signal and gather kids together to move on to your next activity.

GARDEN OF EATIN'
(up to 10 minutes)

Serve kids fruit punch, fresh fruit kabobs, and cut-up vegetables with dip. Let kids rest and enjoy their snacks for about ten minutes, then give the signal and move on to your next activity.

WHAT DO YOU THINK?
(up to 10 minutes)

Mark a line on the floor with masking tape. Then distribute Bibles and have kids look up Genesis 2:4-23. When everyone has found the passage, ask several volunteers to take turns reading the verses. Assign each volunteer three or four verses.

LINEUPS

p. 6

After kids finish reading the passage, ask the following questions one at a time. For each question, offer both of the answers in the parentheses and then designate one end of the tape to represent each answer. Have kids stand on the tape according to how they'd answer the question. For example, if they think living in paradise would have been really great, they'd stand on the "great" end of the tape. If they think living in paradise would have been really terrible, they'd stand on the "terrible" end of the tape. If they think living in paradise might have been kind of boring but not that bad, they'd stand somewhere in the middle.

After kids have taken their positions, have them discuss their answers with someone who had a different opinion.

● **How do you think it would've felt to live in paradise? Stand on the tape to indicate your answer, then tell a partner what would be so good or bad about living in the Garden of Eden.** (Terrible; great.)

● We had a party in our paradise. Do you think paradise in the Garden of Eden was like one big party? Stand on the tape to indicate your answer, then explain your answer to a partner. (Yes; no.)

● How would your life be different today if we still lived in paradise? Stand on the tape to indicate your answer, then tell a partner what would be better or worse about life in paradise. (Better; worse.)

● Do you think paradise will ever happen again? Stand on the tape to indicate your answer, then tell a partner why or why not. (Yes; no.)

Say: **It must've been exciting for** Adam to live in that beautiful garden, to get to name all the animals, then to see the woman God made to be his friend and companion. Next week we'll find out what happened to that first garden paradise. Let's close by thanking God once more for creating it. I'll say, "Thank you God, for a world that's . . ." and you'll fill in a word that describes God's world. You might say "beautiful," "fun," "big," or "diverse."

Let kids fill in their words, then close by saying, "Thank you God" together.

ROAD SIGN

If you have extra time, ask kids if they'd like to play any of the party games again. Then continue the party until it's time to go.

PARADISE LOST

GENESIS 3

DESTINATION

● Kids will learn that God wants us to obey him.
● Kids will learn determination.

You'll need black crepe paper, tape, a sign that says "Condemned," newspapers, thick black markers, Bibles, four photocopies of the "Banished!" script (p. 30), photocopies of the "Christlike Character-Quality Observation Chart" (p. 9), and scissors.

GEAR

PACKING TIPS

You'll need four teenagers or adults to act out Genesis 3 for your class. Assign roles and give each person a photocopy of the "Banished!" script. Set a time during the week to meet with them and run through the script.

ROAD SIGN

For a little fun and a good characterization of a villainous snake, have your actors check out Sir Hiss in Disney's animated *Robin Hood.*

THE JOURNEY: Day 3

PARADISE CONDEMNED

(up to 5 minutes)

Before kids arrive, use black crepe paper and tape to create an X across the classroom door. In the center of the X, attach a sign that says "Condemned." As kids arrive, keep them outside until everyone has arrived. When everyone has arrived, take kids into the classroom.

BANISHED!

(up to 25 minutes)

Station the volunteer who's playing the Angel just inside the door. Have the Angel stop the kids as directed in the "Banished!" script. Read your lines, then follow along in the script as your volunteers replay Genesis 3. After your actors have left the room, say: **Well, you heard them. No more paradise. I guess we'll have to tear all this stuff down.**

Ignore kids' protests and re-emphasize that they must tear down the paradise they've created. Tell them that not one piece of what they've created should remain. After everything is torn down, ask:

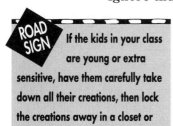

If the kids in your class are young or extra sensitive, have them carefully take down all their creations, then lock the creations away in a closet or cupboard.

● **How did it feel to tear down paradise?** (Rotten; bad; like we did all that work for nothing.)

● **How do you think Adam and Eve felt when they lost their paradise?** (Confused; mad at the snake; sad to leave the garden.)

● **Because of what Adam and Eve did, paradise is gone forever. None of** us will ever know what it was like to live there. **Do you think that's fair or unfair? Explain.** (Not fair, if I'd been there I wouldn't have listened to the snake; fair, because I've disobeyed God too.)

Say: **God created people to love and follow him. When Adam and Eve chose to eat the fruit instead of following God's directions, they stopped following God. It was like they were saying, "God, we don't need you." Before Adam and Eve ate the fruit, God's world was perfect. Their actions introduced sin into the world. Let's look at how the world would be different if Adam and Eve hadn't sinned and disobeyed God.**

As kids prepare to work in groups, review the determination cross chart you made during the first segment of this journey. Remind kids that they need to help each other focus on and meet their goal.

EXTRA! EXTRA!

(up to 15 minutes)

Form groups of four. Give each group a newspaper and a thick black marker. Say: **I'd like you to go through your newspaper and cross out every headline that wouldn't have happened if sin had never entered the world. For example, you might cross out headlines about murder, war, or child abuse.**

p. 7

Have each group choose a reader to read headlines from the newspaper, a marker to cross out the headlines, an encourager to make sure everyone participates, and a

Use a photocopy of the "Christlike Character-Quality Observation Chart" (p. 9) to monitor kids' determination during the "Extra! Extra!" activity. At the end of class, report on positive examples of determination you observed.

PAIR SHARE

p. 6

reporter to share the group's marked newspaper with the class.

After 10 minutes, use your signal to get children's attention. Then have groups each share their changed newspapers.

After all groups have shared, have kids each pair up with someone from another group and discuss the following questions. Pause after you ask each question to allow time for kids to discuss it.

● **What kinds of headlines did your group cross out?** (Murders; robberies; child abuse; war.)

● **What kinds of headlines were left in your newspaper?** (Scientific discoveries; stories about people helping each other; stories about natural disasters; advertisements.)

● **How did Adam and Eve's decision to disobey God change our world?** (Now people think it's OK to disobey God; we don't get to live in paradise; there's a lot of violence.)

● **How do people today change our world when they disobey God?** (All the violence makes it unsafe; families fall apart when parents get divorced; people hurt and kill each other.)

● **Why does God want us to obey him?** (Because he loves us; because he knows what's best for us; because he made us.)

Say: **God wants us to obey him because he loves us and knows what's best for us. When we sin and disobey God, sad things happen. We can't get close to God because our sin gets in the way. When we sin, we hurt God, we hurt ourselves, and sometimes we hurt other people. Sin is a big problem that's been around since Adam**

and Eve. Let's find out how God handles our sin.

A WAY OUT

(up to 15 minutes)

Say: **God let Adam and Eve choose whether or not to obey him. God lets us choose whether or not to obey him, too. Sometimes we choose to obey God, but sometimes we choose to sin and disobey like Adam and Eve did. Let's see what the Bible says about our sin.**

Distribute Bibles and have kids look up Romans 6:23. When everyone has found the passage, ask a volunteer to read it.

Say: **According to this verse, we all deserve to die for our sins. But we don't have to because Jesus died in our place.**

Have children each go to the black crepe paper on the door and cut out a cross. Then have them return with their crosses and sit in a circle on the floor.

ROAD SIGN

You may want to take down the crepe paper and cut it into several pieces to make it easier for kids to cut their crosses.

Read Romans 5:18. Say: **Sin entered the world when Adam and Eve disobeyed God, and people have been disobeying God ever since. Because we are sinful and God is perfect, we could never have a close relationship with God. God knew this, so he sent Jesus to die for us. When Jesus died for us, he took our sin away so we can have a close relationship with God.**

Let's take a moment to thank God for sending Jesus. Take your cross and go to the area of the room where your creation used to be.

Pause for children to go to their areas,

then continue: **Look at your cross and think about what it represents as you quietly pray and thank God for sending Jesus. In a few moments, I'll close.**

Allow a few moments for kids to pray, then close with a prayer similar to this one: **Dear God, thanks for sending Jesus to forgive us for our sins. We're glad we can have a close relationship with you. Help us to honor and obey you in all we do this week. In Jesus' name, amen.**

Have kids take their crosses home or tape them to the wall of your room to remind you of your Genesis journey. Encourage any children who'd like to know more about the meaning of Christ's life and death to talk to you after class. Also, give groups their "Christlike Character-Quality Observation Charts" and praise them for the determination they showed during this journey.

BANISHED!

(Angel stands near the door, arms crossed, looking stern. Adam and Eve stand or kneel behind a door, bookcase, or other large object. If this isn't possible, they should stand in a corner, facing the wall. Snake hides somewhere in the room.)

ANGEL: Stop! I'm sorry, but I can't let you in here.

TEACHER: What do you mean you can't let us in? This is our room—we've worked hard to create our own garden paradise, and we want to come in and enjoy it.

ANGEL: I'm sorry, but this paradise has been condemned. No one is allowed to come in. You can see that Adam and Eve have gone.

TEACHER: What happened? Where are they?
(Adam and Eve appear, hanging their heads sadly.)

ADAM AND EVE: Here we are.

ANGEL: Hey! I thought I told you two to get out of here. God wants you to leave. Now scram!

ADAM: We're leaving, but first we'd like to tell them what happened.

ANGEL: OK, but make it quick.

EVE: *(Walking around looking at and touching kids' creations)* We were having such a good time in the garden. Each day we'd walk around and enjoy all the animals and plants God made. Then one day I met this snake.

SNAKE: *(Holding up a snake kids have created, speaking in a wily voice)* Hisss. I heard that God won't let you eat any of the fruit in this garden. Hisss. Is that true?

EVE: We can eat fruit from any tree except the tree that's in the middle of the garden. God said if we eat fruit from that tree, we'd die.

SNAKE: Hisss. You won't die. God knows that if you eat that fruit you'll learn about good *(coughs)* and evil. Hisss. Then you'll be like God.

EVE: Well, it does look good. *(Eve reaches up and pretends to pick a piece of fruit as the Snake watches gleefully. She takes a bite, then picks several more pieces. The Snake watches her pick the fruit, then slithers away.)*

EVE: I'll just take some of this fruit to Adam. *(She gives Adam a piece of the fruit and eats another one herself.)*

ADAM: Everything was fine until God came down to the garden. We were so ashamed, we hid from him. But it was no use. God knew where we were, and he knew that we'd eaten the fruit.

EVE: I tried to blame it on that nasty snake, but God punished us anyway.

ADAM: God said we'd have to leave this beautiful garden. We won't be able to just pick fruit from the trees for food. We'll have to work hard to grow food to eat.

EVE: Because we disobeyed God, we lost our paradise. Come, Adam, we must go.

(Angel escorts Adam and Eve out of the room. Snake follows, hissing triumphantly.)

Journey Through EXODUS

"I will go to Egypt with you,
and I will bring you out of Egypt again."
GENESIS 46:4A

The Israelites' presence in Egypt began in the time of Joseph. After Joseph revealed himself to his brothers, he invited them to return with their father, Jacob. As Jacob was traveling to Egypt, God spoke to him in a vision and promised to go with him to this strange, new land. Old Jacob probably had no idea his descendants would live in Egypt for nearly 400 years!

Years of torturous slavery made Jacob's descendants doubt that God really cared for them. When the Israelites cried out for help, they didn't expect God to hear them. But God did. God raised up Moses to lead his people out of Egypt, just as he'd promised Jacob years before. And as the Israelites traveled out of Egypt, God went with them. God parted the sea, provided food and water, and traveled alongside them as a pillar of cloud or fire. Each day, the Israelites experienced God's faithfulness.

This five-week journey leads kids through the book of Exodus, the record of Israel's journey out of Egypt. Kids will form Hebrew families and work as slaves in Egypt. They'll share a Passover meal together and escape Pharaoh's armies by crossing the Red Sea. Then they'll learn about God's rules, the Ten Commandments, and why they're important.

Kids today have their own reasons to doubt God's faithfulness. Parents divorce, friends turn away, and kids often find themselves alone with their hurts. They find it difficult to believe that God is faithful. This journey will help kids experience firsthand what the Israelites felt as God met their needs. Kids will understand that God is the same yesterday, today, and forever and that he's faithful to meet their needs, too.

Set up your room to make it look and feel like a desert. Come up with your own decoration ideas or use one or more of the following ideas:

● Place a large fan in each corner of the room to create swirling winds.

● On each wall, paint a paper mural with camels, cactuses, tents, and swirling dust. You could even create a mirage with aluminum foil, cellophane, or Mylar.

● Turn up the heat in your room so it really feels like a desert.

THE ISRAELITES' SUFFERING

EXODUS 1-3

DESTINATION

- Kids will learn that God is faithful.
- Kids will learn teamwork.

GEAR

For every four kids you'll need one set of "Hebrew-Family Cards" (pp. 39-40); a full-sized, light-colored bedsheet; scissors; and a large, empty appliance box. You'll also need photocopies of the "Christlike Character-Quality Observation Chart" (p. 9), newsprint, a marker, tape, a 3-foot piece of rope or twine for each child, photocopies of the "Tunic Pattern" (p. 38), yarn or string, scissors, a utility knife, and Bibles.

PACKING TIPS

- Don't forget to select a signal!
- Most of the gear for this journey can be found around your home or church. However, you'll need to do extra legwork to get the bedsheets and appliance boxes. Months in advance of this journey, ask church members to donate old bedsheets and to save empty appliance boxes.

ROAD SIGN

If you've used other journeys in this book, you may want to vary the "Prepare With Prayer" introduction. But keep in mind that you may have students who haven't heard the information before. If you do vary the introduction, don't forget to start out with prayer.

THE JOURNEY: Day 1

PREPARE WITH PRAYER

(up to 5 minutes)

Say: **Today marks the start of an exciting adventure for our class. We're going to be learning about events that happened long ago in Bible times. But we're not just going to read or talk about them; we're going to create a Bible-times environment right here in our classroom and experience Bible events as if we were actually there. It will be like taking a journey back to Bible times.**

Ask:

● **When have you taken a journey?** (When I went to my grandma's for Thanksgiving; when our family went on vacation; when my scout troop went camping.)

● **What was your favorite part of the journey?** (Flying in an airplane; coming home to my friends; seeing my cousins.)

● **What new things did you discover on the journey?** (I learned how to put up a tent; I saw a bald eagle; I went to three states I'd never been to before.)

Say: **Journeys are a lot of fun. We get to be with our family or friends, and we get to do fun things and see new places. Sometimes we learn new things when we go on journeys. During our journey back to Bible times, we'll be learning new things about God and about each other. We'll have to work together and help each other along the way. Let's ask God to help us do that.**

Pray: **Dear God, thanks for giving us** the Bible to help us learn about you. **Please be with us as we go on our journey. Help us work together as we learn new things. In Jesus' name, amen.**

DESTINATION: TEAMWORK

(up to 5 minutes)

Say: **Our Bible journey is going to take us back to the time of the Exodus. We'll learn how God led his people out of Egypt and provided for their needs in the wilderness. As we go on our journey together, we'll also be learning teamwork. What do you know about teamwork?** (Let kids respond.)

Say: **Teamwork means working together with others to achieve a goal. If you've ever played on a sports team, you know about teamwork. Everyone on the team plays a different position, but you all work together to try to win the game.**

Ask:

● **What other examples of teamwork can you think of?** (Singing in the choir; playing in a band or orchestra; fixing dinner together.)

● **Why is teamwork important?** (Everyone gets to participate; some jobs don't seem so big or hard when people work together; it's more fun.)

Say: **As we go on our journey together, be thinking of ways you can show teamwork. To help us remember about teamwork, let's make a chart.**

Post a sheet of newsprint and draw a cross chart as described on page 8. Write "teamwork" above the cross.

Say: **We're making this chart in the shape of a cross to remind us that Jesus showed teamwork, too. Jesus worked together with his disciples when he was here on earth. On the left side of the cross, let's write what teamwork sounds like. What kinds of things would you hear people say if they're showing teamwork?**

List kids' responses on the newsprint. They may say that teamwork sounds like "We can do it," "Let's figure this out," or "Yea, team!"

Say: **On the right side of the cross, let's write what teamwork looks like. What kinds of things would you see people doing if they're showing teamwork?**

List kids' responses on the newsprint. They may say that teamwork looks like kids working together, everyone contributing and talking, or being excited when the team succeeds.

Say: **As we go on our journey, you can use this chart to help you remember to practice teamwork. I'll be looking at our chart, too, and watching for people or groups who are showing teamwork.**

FAMILY TIME

(up to 10 minutes)

p. 7

Before class, photocopy and cut apart the "Hebrew-Family Cards" (pp. 39-40). Randomly distribute the cards. Say: **We'll be working in family groups on our Exodus journey. I've given each of you a Hebrew-family card. You'll need to find the other people who have the same card. Hold your card up high as you walk around the room and call out the name that's written on it. When** you've found everyone who has the same card, sit down together.

When all the kids have gathered in their family groups, have groups take turns standing up and giving their family names (Reuben, Judah, Zebulun, etc.).

After all the families have introduced themselves, say: **We're going to be learning what life might have been like at the time of the Exodus, when God's people left Egypt. But first, let's see what we already know about Exodus. Go around your group and take turns telling what you know about what happened to God's people when they were slaves in Egypt. You could also tell something you know about Egypt. For example, you might say that God's people had to make bricks or that Egypt is a country in Africa.**

After several minutes, give the signal to let kids know they need to wrap up their family discussions. Invite representatives from each family to report on their discussions. List things kids know about Egypt and the Exodus on a sheet of newsprint. Then say: **As we go on our journey, we'll be learning more about Egypt and what it was like for God's people to live there. I'll post this list in our room, and as we learn more, you can add to it.**

> **ROAD SIGN**
>
> If new kids join your class in the middle of a journey, add them to an existing family group. It's OK if some family groups have three or five members. Welcoming newcomers is more important than having ideal group sizes.

FAMILY CHORES

(up to 25 minutes)

Have kids remain in their family groups and work together to create a house for their families and a tunic for each member. Encourage kids to share responsibilities and help each other as they complete both projects.

Say: **To help you feel more like Israelite families, you'll be working together to make a house for your family. You'll also make tunics to wear during our journey.**

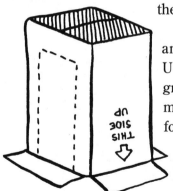

ROAD SIGN As a preview to the next activity, take on the role of a taskmaster. As kids work, circulate around the room to monitor their progress. From time to time, remind them that they have a lot of work to do and encourage them to work harder and faster on their houses and tunics.

Give each family group a full-sized bedsheet, a pair of sharp scissors, and a photocopy of the "Tunic Pattern" (p. 38). Have groups cut their bedsheets into four square sections. Using the pattern as a guide, help kids make a tunic for each group member.

After kids have finished and tried on their tunics, give them each a piece of twine or rope to use as a belt. Tell kids that they'll need to leave their tunics in class and wear them each week of the journey.

Provide each group with an empty appliance box. Using a utility knife, help groups each cut a door to make the box into a house for themselves. See the illustration in the margin to help you guide kids in their home building.

After kids have cut their doors, have them decorate their houses.

When you're about ready to move on to the next activity, have family groups gather in or around their houses.

ROAD SIGN Don't worry if kids don't completely finish their houses during this meeting. As kids arrive early or have free time during other meetings on this journey, they can work on decorating their houses.

BREAK THESE CHAINS
(up to 5 minutes)

Say: **Let's see what it might have felt like for the Israelites to be slaves. I'll pretend to be the master, and you can all pretend to be the slaves. I'll start by calling the roll. When I call your family name, please report for work.**

After you've called all the families to report, have kids sit in a tight clump on the floor. Using yarn or string, tie kids together in one large group. After you've tied kids together, walk around the clump ranting and raving and calling out orders and complaints about your "slaves' " work. Be overly dramatic so kids know it's an act.

You may want to say things such as "You only made 65 bricks? That's not enough!" or "Tomorrow you'll have to work even harder!"

After about a minute, untie kids and apologize for treating them as your slaves. Ask:

● **What thoughts went through your mind as you had to listen to me yelling at you?** (It made me mad; I didn't like it even though I knew you weren't really our boss; I wanted to break the string and get away.)

● **How was your experience just now like or unlike the slavery the Israelites experienced in Egypt?** (Theirs was worse because they really were slaves; their masters were probably meaner than you; they probably felt like they couldn't escape just like we couldn't escape when we were tied together.)

● **The Israelites lived in Egypt for about 400 years. As long as they could remember, they had been slaves. How would you feel about God** if God allowed you to be a slave all of your life? (Mad; like it wasn't fair; I'd pray and ask God to do something about it.)

Say: **The book of Exodus tells us that the Egyptians made the Israelites' lives bitter. Slave labor was hard and painful, and it's easy to see why the Israelites might have been angry at God for allowing the Egyptians to make their lives so miserable. As we continue on our journey, we'll learn how God was faithful to help the Israelites out of their misery.**

WORD OF A DELIVERER

(up to 10 minutes)

Whisper the following statement in one child's ear: "God is sending a deliverer. We won't be slaves anymore! Pass it on." Have kids continue passing the message until everyone has heard it.

Once everyone has heard the message, have kids sit near their houses with their families. Ask kids to tell you the message they heard. Repeat the original message if necessary to correct any garbled messages kids may have heard. Ask:

● **How do you think the Israelites felt when they heard they wouldn't be slaves anymore?** (They probably didn't believe it at first; they felt like celebrating; really glad and relieved.)

● **When have you felt some of those feelings?** (When school gets out; when I made the soccer team; when you untied us earlier.)

Say: **The Israelites had been slaves for so long, it was probably hard for them to believe that God was sending a deliverer to set them free. Let's look in our Bibles to find out how that happened. Look up and read Exodus** ▼

3:1-15 **with your group, and in a few minutes I'll ask you some questions about it.**

Make sure each group has at least one Bible. When kids have finished reading, ask the following questions one at a time. Have kids form pairs or trios within their family groups to discuss them. Ask:

● **What do you think Moses thought when he saw the burning bush and heard the voice coming from it?** (That he was going crazy; he wondered why the bush didn't burn up; he knew something strange was going on.)

● **How did Moses respond when God asked him to lead the people out of Egypt?** (He was scared; he didn't know what to say; he was glad God promised to be with him.)

● **If you were Moses, how would you have responded?** (I would have tried to put out the fire; I would have asked for help; I would have been just as scared as Moses was.)

Say: **Moses knew it would be hard to get the king of Egypt to free the Israelites, but he also knew God would be faithful to help him.**

Ask:

● **What are some hard areas in your life God can help you with this week?** (Getting along with my sister; understanding my math homework; keeping my temper under control.)

After kids have discussed the last question, give the signal to bring everyone together. Invite kids to share the responses they gave in their groups. Then have kids stand in a circle. Say: **Even though the Israelites were God's chosen people, they still went through struggles and hard times—especially while they** were slaves in Egypt. As God's people today, we have hard times, too. Let's pray and ask God to help us in the hard times we just talked about.

Pray: **Dear God, thanks for being such a faithful helper. We know you'll help us with our hard times just like you helped the Israelites. Help us to trust your faithfulness this week. In Jesus' name, amen.**

Before kids leave, point out any positive examples of teamwork you noticed. Refer to the cross chart or fill out a "Christlike Character-Quality Observation Chart" (p. 9). Then remind kids to leave their tunics in the classroom. Encourage them to come back next week to continue the journey.

Tunic Pattern

Fold each bedsheet section in half. Cut a neck hole and an opening down the front as shown.

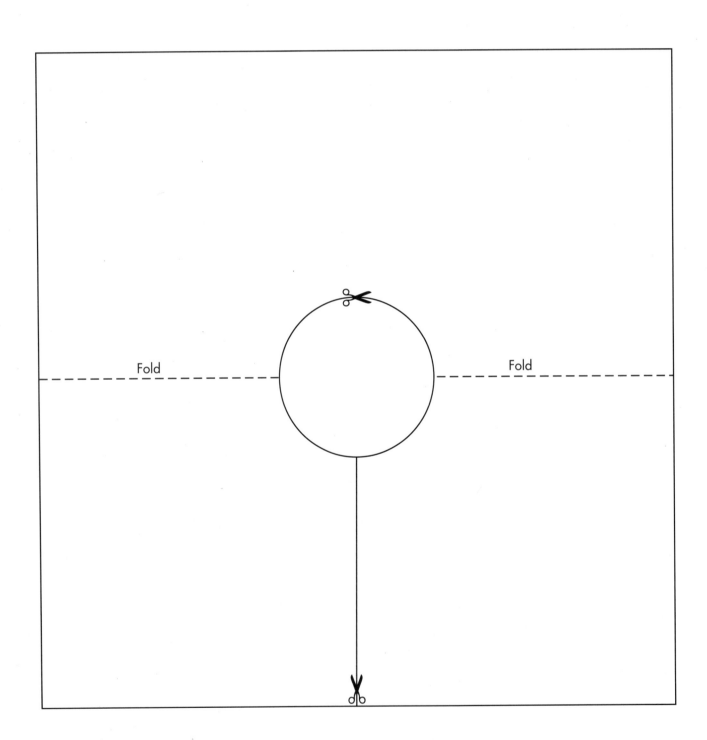

HEBREW-FAMILY CARDS

Photocopy and cut apart these cards. Each name represents one Hebrew family. If you have a large class, use all the names to create up to nine families. If you have a small class, you'll only need two or three different names.

Reuben	Reuben	Reuben	Reuben
Judah	Judah	Judah	Judah
Zebulun	Zebulun	Zebulun	Zebulun
Issachar	Issachar	Issachar	Issachar
Dan	Dan	Dan	Dan

Hebrew-Family Cards
continued

Asher	**Asher**	**Asher**	**Asher**
Naphtali	**Naphtali**	**Naphtali**	**Naphtali**
Joseph	Joseph	Joseph	Joseph
Benjamin	**Benjamin**	**Benjamin**	**Benjamin**

PLAGUES AND DELIVERANCE

EXODUS 6-12

- Kids will learn that God is faithful.
- Kids will learn teamwork.

For each family group, you'll need a flashlight and a photocopy of the "Hebrew Alphabet" handout (p. 45). You'll also need Bibles; photocopies of the "Christlike Character-Quality Observation Chart" (p. 9); a photocopy of the "Plagues, Plagues, Plagues!" handout (p. 46); scissors; markers; a flashlight covered with red transparent paper; a bowl of washable, red tempera paint; paintbrushes; paper plates or napkins; lamb; matzo or another unleavened bread; horseradish; paper cups; and grape juice.

The "Passover Meal" activity will take extra preparation. You can purchase matzo in the international section of most grocery stores. You'll need to call ahead to find out where you can purchase lamb. If your local grocery store doesn't carry it, you should be able to get it from a butcher or a meat market. Lamb chops cook quickly, and you can buy one chop for each family group in your class. Cook lamb chops in the broiler for about 15 minutes, then cut them into bite-sized pieces.

If kids arrive early, have them continue to work on their houses.

ROAD SIGN

If you know someone who's Jewish or you feel comfortable calling your local synagogue, you can find out more about the Jewish celebration of Passover. If not, you can simply follow the Passover directions outlined in this journey, which are based on the traditional celebration of Passover.

THE JOURNEY: Day 2

FAMILY TIME

(up to 15 minutes)

LEARNING GROUP
p. 7

When kids arrive, have them get with their family groups and put on their tunics. Show kids the teamwork cross chart they made last week. Review the "sounds like" side and the "looks like" side. Ask kids if they'd like to add anything to either side. Then remind them that you'll be looking for positive ways they work as a team with their family groups.

Give each group markers and a photocopy of the "Hebrew Alphabet" handout (p. 45). Say: **Work with your family members to design a family-name symbol for your house. You can use any combination of English letters, pictures, or letters from the "Hebrew Alphabet" handout.**

After about 10 minutes, give the signal to regain kids' attention. Have groups present their family-name symbols to the class. After groups have all presented their symbols, say: **Today we're going to discover what happened when Moses tried to lead all the Israelite families out of Egypt.**

ROAD SIGN

As groups work, use a photocopy of the "Christ-like Character-Quality Observation Chart" (p. 9) to monitor how well they're working as a team. Use a separate observation chart for each group. Be sure to watch for things you listed on your teamwork cross chart. Note positive examples of teamwork and point out one or two areas where groups can make their teamwork even stronger. Set the completed charts aside until the end of class.

LITANY OF PLAGUES

JIGSAW
p. 7

(up to 15 minutes)

Before class, photocopy the "Plagues, Plagues, Plagues!" handout (p. 46) and cut it apart. Post one section in each corner of the room. Have family members number off from one to four. Send all the ones to one corner of the room, the twos to another corner, the threes to a third corner, and the fours to the last corner. When kids have assembled in their assigned corners, say: **I've put a different set of instructions in each corner. Work with the people in your corner to follow your instructions. You'll be reading and talking about what happened in Egypt when the Israelites got ready to leave. After a few minutes, you'll return to your family group. Then you'll get a chance to share what you learned in your corner with your group.**

After about 10 minutes, use the signal to send kids back to their family groups. Have kids each pantomime and explain the plagues they learned about. Then give the signal again and wait for kids to respond. Say: **When Moses asked Pharaoh to let the Israelites go, he refused. So God turned the river water to blood and then sent plagues of frogs, gnats, flies, diseases, hail, locusts, and darkness. But God was faithful to protect the Israelites. No hail fell on their crops; none of their animals got sick. Even when God said that all the first-born sons in Egypt would die, he told**

ROAD SIGN

Circulate between corners to offer help as necessary. Some plagues, such as frogs and locusts, will be easy for kids to pantomime. Others, such as boils and darkness, could be difficult. Encourage kids who are pantomiming boils to pretend they're sick, scratch themselves, or even draw spots on their arms with washable markers. Encourage kids who are pantomiming darkness to pretend they're sleeping, fumble around as if they can't see, or turn off the classroom lights.

the Israelites how they'd be saved. Let's find out how that happened.

WEEPING AND WAILING

(up to 15 minutes)

p. 7

Have family groups huddle around their houses, then turn off the classroom lights. Create "firelight" by setting a flashlight covered with red transparent paper in the center of the room. Give each group its own flashlight and a Bible.

Say: **It's a terrible night in Egypt. All across the land, firstborn sons are dying. You wonder if your house will be the next to be struck by this terrible plague. But you know God is faithful. He's protected you and your family from other plagues, and he can protect you from this one. Read Exodus 12:21-30 to figure out how God will protect your family.**

As kids are reading the passage, quietly set out a bowl of red paint and paintbrushes. Encourage kids to paint the "blood" above the doors of their houses so the angel of death will pass over.

After all the kids have painted their door frames, put the paint and paintbrushes away and collect kids' flashlights. Have family groups gather in front of their houses and pray for God's protection. Close the prayer time with a prayer similar to this one: **Dear God, you protected the Israelites, and we know you'll protect us, too. Thank you for your faithful protection in our lives. Help us to trust you even when we're scared. In Jesus' name, amen.**

PASSOVER MEAL

(up to 20 minutes)

Say: **Jewish people have been cele-** brating Passover for hundreds of years to help them remember God's faithfulness. Celebrating Passover can help Christians remember God's faithfulness, too. As we eat some of the traditional Passover foods, you'll have a chance to tell your group members about times God has been faithful to you.

When it's time to stop talking and move on to the next Passover food, I'll raise my hand. When you see me raise my hand, you raise your hands. When I see that everyone's hand is up, I'll know I have your attention and we'll move on. Now listen as I read about Passover from the Bible.

Read aloud Exodus 12:1-4, 8, 11-14. Then give each family group paper plates or napkins and a portion of lamb. Say: **This lamb reminds us of the plague we just experienced. When God saw the lamb's blood over the Israelites' doors, he "passed over" their homes and spared their firstborn sons. As you take your piece of lamb, tell your group members about a time God protected you or someone you know.**

After kids have eaten their lamb, raise your hand and wait for kids to raise their hands. Give each family a piece of matzo bread. Say: **The unleavened bread reminds us that the Israelites had to leave Egypt in a hurry. They didn't even have time for their bread dough to rise. Pretend you're an Israelite. As you take a piece of unleavened bread, tell your family members how you feel about leaving Egypt.**

ROAD SIGN

Use your judgment about lighting conditions during this activity. Keep the lights low if you think it will help kids maintain a serious, reflective mood. If you think kids will get silly or disrespectful in the darkness, turn the lights back on.

After kids have eaten their matzo, raise your hand and wait for kids to raise their hands. Hold up a bowl of horseradish. Say: **This bitter herb reminds us that the Egyptians made the lives of the Israelites bitter by forcing them to be slaves. Go around your circle and say one word that describes how you would feel if you had to work hard as a slave.**

After a few moments, raise your hand and wait for kids to raise their hands. Give each family group a spoonful of horseradish and tell them to pass it around and have each person dip one finger in it to taste it. Say: **As you taste the bitterness of slavery, thank God for the gift of freedom. You can say, "Thanks for freedom," "God, I'm glad we're free," or simply "Thank you, God." When everyone in your group has tasted the bitter herbs, come and join me in the center of the room. Be sure to walk quietly, so you don't disturb other groups.**

When all the kids have gathered in the center, raise your hand and wait for them to raise their hands. Begin pouring grape juice into paper cups and handing the

ROAD SIGN
If some kids don't want to taste the horseradish, encourage them to pass it quietly to the next person. If kids make faces or complain that the horseradish is "yucky," remind them to think about how "yucky" it was for the Israelites to be slaves in Egypt.

filled cups to the kids. As you're pouring, say: **God poured out 10 plagues on Egypt before Pharaoh finally let the Israelites go. Before we drink this juice, let's remember those plagues.**

Lead kids in recalling the 10 plagues they learned about earlier. After you've recounted all 10 plagues, say: **As you drink your juice, thank God that he not only delivered the Israelites from the punishment of the plagues, but that, through Jesus, he's faithful to deliver us from the punishment for the wrong things we do.**

ROAD SIGN
If you need help remembering the 10 plagues, refer to this list:

1. Water turns to blood
2. Frogs
3. Gnats
4. Flies
5. Disease of farm animals
6. Boils
7. Hail
8. Locusts
9. Darkness
10. Death of firstborn sons

Have kids drink their juice, then collect the cups. Close by singing a praise song your kids know, such as "God Is So Good," "Steadfast Love," or "The Doxology."

Give groups their "Christlike Character-Quality Observation Charts." As they're waiting for their parents to arrive, have them discuss ways they can work better as a team next week. Remind kids to leave their tunics in the classroom and encourage them to return next week when you'll flee Egypt.

HEBREW ALPHABET

Modern Hebrew Alphabet	English Equivalent	Modern Hebrew Alphabet	English Equivalent
א	'Aleph*	ל	l
ב	b	מ	m
ג	g	נ	n
ד	d	ס	c
ה	h	ע	'Ayin**
ו	v or w	פ	p
ז	z	צ	ts
ח	ch	ק	q
ט	t	ר	r
י	y	שׁ	sh
כ	k	ת	th

* silent
** no English equivalent

PLAGUES, PLAGUES, PLAGUES!

READ EXODUS 7:14–8:19.

- What do you think the Egyptians thought about these plagues?
- How did Pharaoh respond to these plagues?
- What would it be like if these plagues happened today?

Work together to create motions you can use to act out these plagues for your family groups.

READ EXODUS 8:20–9:12.

- What do you think the Egyptians thought about these plagues?
- How did Pharaoh respond to these plagues?
- What would it be like if these plagues happened today?

Work together to create motions you can use to act out these plagues for your family groups.

READ EXODUS 9:13–10:20.

- What do you think the Egyptians thought about these plagues?
- How did Pharaoh respond to these plagues?
- What would it be like if these plagues happened today?

Work together to create motions you can use to act out these plagues for your family groups.

READ EXODUS 10:21–11:10.

- What do you think the Egyptians thought about these plagues?
- How did Pharaoh respond to these plagues?
- What would it be like if these plagues happened today?

Work together to create motions you can use to act out these plagues for your family groups.

3

WE'RE OUTTA HERE!

EXODUS 12:37-15:21

- Kids will learn that God is faithful.
- Kids will learn teamwork.

You'll need several photocopies of the "Spoils" handout (p. 51), scissors, three to five teenage or adult volunteers, a large sheet of black plastic (the kind used in gardens, available at nurseries and hardware stores), wide masking tape, two electric fans, Bibles, paper, pencils, envelopes, photocopies of the "How's It Going?" handout (p. 10), matzo or unleavened bread, water, and paper cups.

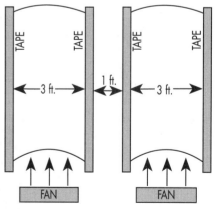

In a vacant room, make a "Red Sea" out of plastic, masking tape, and fans. Cut out two 4×5-foot lengths of black plastic. Lay the pieces of plastic on the floor as shown in the diagram at the right. The pieces should be about a foot apart. Tape the plastic to the floor as shown, then set a fan at the end of each piece of plastic. The fans should be facing the plastic. You'll be using the fans to "billow" the plastic "sea." Make sure you don't stretch the plastic too tightly, or it won't blow. Read how you'll be using the Red Sea on page 49, then test your Red Sea a few times so you can make any necessary adjustments well in advance of this week's journey.

Make sure others in your church know not to disturb your sea. If you set the room up during the week, you may need to place a Do Not Disturb sign on the door.

Arrange a time to meet with your volunteers. Explain that they'll be playing the part of Pharaoh's army. Agree on a place in the church for them to hide. When your

"Israelites" pass by the army's hiding place, the volunteers must run out and chase children to the room where you've set up the Red Sea. Remind your volunteers to chase the Israelites from a safe distance. Kids should feel like they're being pursued, but volunteers shouldn't be close enough to catch them.

Be sure your volunteers know the location of the Red Sea room. After the kids are all inside the room, volunteers must pound on the door and call out threats such as "We'll get you Israelites!" or "You can't escape!" When you open the door, they'll walk into the room and through the sea. As you turn the fans on them, they'll pretend to drown in the sea. Encourage them to dramatize the experience by saying things such as "Help! We're drowning!" or "I wish I'd never joined Pharaoh's army."

THE JOURNEY: Day 3

GETTING READY

(up to 10 minutes)

p. 7

Before class, make photocopies of the "Spoils" handout (p. 51) and cut apart the cards. You'll need enough photocopies for each family group to receive six cards.

When kids arrive, have them get with their family groups and put on their tunics. Show kids the teamwork cross chart. Review the "sounds like" side and the "looks like" side. Point out positive examples of teamwork you noticed in previous parts of the journey. Then set out the "spoils" cards on the floor.

Say: **The Egyptians are so eager to get rid of you and to stop the plagues that they'll give you anything you want. Decide in your groups which six cards you want to take on your journey. Remember that there won't be any stores along the way, and this could be a very difficult journey. So choose wisely. You must all agree on each item you choose. In addition to your six cards, your family group will get a bowl of un-leavened bread, a cart, and a tent.**

After groups have selected their cards, have each group put its family name on an envelope and place its cards in it. Collect the envelopes for use during the last week of this journey.

OFF WE GO

(up to 10 minutes)

Say: **It's time to go! We're ready to leave Egypt. Families, your houses are now your carts. Load up your supplies and line up with your carts by the door.**

Have families pretend to load supplies into their carts. After they've all loaded their carts and lined up, give the signal and wait for kids to respond. Say: **God is faithful. As God promised, he is leading us out of slavery. We must hurry and follow him.**

Have families pick up their carts and follow you as they march through or

ROAD SIGN

If you're using a noisemaker as a signal, be sure to take it with you when you leave the room. You'll need it for the next activity.

around the church. As you march, encourage kids to call out, "We're leaving Egypt!" or "We're finally free!"

After about five minutes, lead them by the place where your volunteer Egyptians are hiding. Have the volunteers jump out and chase the kids just as the real Egyptians pursued the Israelites. As the Egyptians begin to chase you, yell: **Oh no! Pharaoh has sent his army after us! Run!**

Let the Egyptians chase the kids for a minute (or several minutes if you're outside). Then lead kids to the Red Sea room you've prepared for the next activity.

ROAD SIGN Plan your "escape route" ahead of time so you can minimize disruption to other classes. If the weather's nice, have your volunteers hide outdoors so they can really chase the kids. If you have to stay indoors and you know you'll be passing by other classes, be sure to warn the teachers ahead of time. Most teachers won't mind putting up with a brief disruption if they know what your kids are doing.

WHAT TO DO?
(up to 5 minutes)

PAIR SHARE
◗ ◖
p. 6

Run into the Red Sea room and close the door. Have the Egyptians pound on the door and yell threats to your Israelites. Have them keep pounding and yelling intermittently until you open the door.

As you stand at the edge of the Red Sea, have kids turn to a partner and answer the following questions. Pause after you ask each question to allow time for pairs to discuss it. Ask:

● **How do you feel right now?** (Tired; excited; curious about the plastic on the floor.)

● **How do you think the Israelites felt when the Egyptians came after them?** (They were scared; they wished they could run faster; they wondered if God would save them.)

After pairs have discussed the last ques-

tion, give the signal and wait for kids to respond. Then ask the entire group:

● **What should we do now?** (Stay here for the rest of our class; walk over the plastic; open the door and face the Egyptians.)

Say: **God is faithful! God will lead us through the Red Sea!**

CROSSING THE SEA
(up to 10 minutes)

Turn on the fans so the plastic billows up. Lead kids through the Red Sea. Then open the door and have the Egyptians follow through the sea. Just as the Egyptians enter the sea, rip up the outside tape and turn the fans toward the Egyptians so the plastic blows all over them. The Egyptians will be swallowed up by the plastic sea. Stand by and watch until the Egyptians are all lying on the floor.

Say: **We did it! We escaped from the Egyptians! God has delivered us from slavery!**

Have kids congratulate each other with cheers or high fives, then lead them

ROAD SIGN You may want to have someone help you rip up the tape so it can be done quickly. Station an additional adult or teenage helper in this room or plan ahead to have one of the Egyptians "defect."

back to your classroom for the rest of this part of the journey. Be sure groups take their carts back with them.

DELIVERED
(up to 15 minutes)

Have family groups gather by their carts. Make sure each group has a Bible. Say: **Moses and the Israelites were so happy to be free, they made up a song to sing to God. Let's read their song together.**

Assign each group one or two verses

ROUND TABLE
p. 7

from Exodus 15:1-13. Have groups take turns reading the verses aloud. After they've read the whole passage, say: **God was faithful to deliver the Israelites from an impossible situation. In your family groups, tell about a time God was faithful to you or someone you know in a really hard situation. Maybe you moved to a new place and God helped you find good friends, or maybe God helped you stand up to a tough temptation at school.**

After everyone in your group has shared, choose one situation you can all identify with. When your group has chosen a situation, raise your hands, then I'll give you your next set of instructions.

Allow several minutes for kids to share their experiences with God's faithfulness. As you see groups raise their hands, approach them to explain the next part of the activity. Give each group a sheet of paper and a pencil and explain that they'll be writing a song of deliverance like the one they just read in Exodus 15. Instead of thanking God for delivering them from the Red Sea, groups' songs will thank God for being faithful in the situations they've just chosen. Encourage kids to pass the sheet of paper around the group so each member can add a line to the song.

Once groups have finished their songs, have them take turns performing their songs for each other. After the last song, close the activity with a prayer similar to this one: **Dear God, thanks for your great faithfulness. You delivered the Israelites from slavery, and we know you'll always be there to deliver us from tough situations, too. We love you, and we honor you. In Jesus' name, amen.**

YUM, YUM!

(up to 5 minutes)

Serve kids matzo bread and water for refreshments. Ignore any complaints until next week. While family groups are eating, give them each a photocopy of the "How's It Going?" handout (p. 10). Have kids work together to evaluate their groups' teamwork.

As kids leave, collect the "How's It Going?" handouts. Remind kids to leave their tunics in the classroom and encourage them to return for the next part of your journey next week.

ROAD SIGN

Some groups may need help with the song-writing part of this activity. If kids need help with words, encourage them to pick up some of the words from Exodus 15. For example, instead of "I will sing to the Lord, because he is worthy of great honor. He has thrown the horse and its rider into the sea" (Exodus 15:1), kids might write, "I will sing to the Lord, because he is a great God. He helped me say no to peer pressure."

If kids need help with music, encourage them to use tunes from familiar church songs or even nursery rhyme tunes. If worries about music or singing hinder their progress, have kids do a rap instead.

SPOILS

Photocopy this handout and cut out the "spoils" cards. You'll need six cards for each family group.

WANDERERS

EXODUS 16-20

DESTINATION

● Kids will learn that God is faithful.
● Kids will learn teamwork.

GEAR

You'll need photocopies of the "Ten Commandments Today" (p. 56) and "Christlike-Character Awards" (pp. 11-13) handouts. You'll also need matzo or other unleavened bread, water, paper cups, cooked pie-crust strips, cooked chicken wings, Bibles, paper, pencils, and tape.

PACKING TIPS

Photocopy the "Christlike-Character Awards" handout onto colored paper. You'll need at least one teamwork award for each family group. Cut off the other award sections from each handout and save them for use in future lessons.

Photocopy the "Ten Commandments Today" handout and cut it apart. Put one section of the handout in each corner of your classroom.

The pie-crust strips and chicken wings you'll serve in this lesson require a little extra preparation. If you don't cook much or are short on time, try one of the ideas below:

● If you don't have time to prepare your own pie crust, you can purchase already-prepared pie crust in the freezer section of most grocery stores. Thaw the pie crust, then cut it into strips. Bake at 450° until lightly brown.

● Check the freezer section of your grocery store for frozen, precooked chicken wings. Cook them according to the directions on the package. Some grocery store delicatessens also carry prepared chicken wings.

● If you can't get pie-crust strips and chicken wings, improvise with other bread and poultry products. Use crumbled biscuits and chicken legs, shredded croissants and turkey breast, or torn white bread and Cornish hens.

> **ROAD SIGN**
>
> Remind kids to practice teamwork in today's journey. Monitor family groups as they work together. While the kids are working on the "Thou Shalt..." activity, complete at least one teamwork award for each group. Present the awards at the end of class. Kids could post their awards on a classroom bulletin board, if they wish.

THE JOURNEY: Day 4

GET TOGETHER
(up to 5 minutes)

When kids arrive, have them get with their family groups and put on their tunics. Show kids the teamwork cross chart. Review the "sounds like" side and the "looks like" side. Point out the positive examples of teamwork you noticed in previous parts of the journey. Then remind them that you'll be looking for positive ways they work as a team with their family groups.

WHAT'S FOR SUPPER?
(up to 10 minutes)

PAIR SHARE
p. 6

Say: **I thought we'd start our day's journey with some refreshment. We wouldn't want to get hungry and start feeling faint in the middle of our class.**

Serve kids the matzo and water. They'll probably complain about having the same refreshments as last week. If they don't complain, egg them on as you're passing out the meager fare. Say things like "Don't you love matzo!" or "You'll need lots of water so you don't get dehydrated in the wilderness."

After everyone has been served, form pairs. Have partners answer the following questions. Pause after you ask each question to allow time for kids to discuss it. Ask:

● **What thoughts went through your head when you first saw our refreshments?** (Not matzo again; I wish we could have juice or soda instead of water; unleavened bread is cool.)

● **If you could have any kind of refreshments right now, what kind would you choose?** (Cookies; popcorn; pizza; not this kind.)

Give the signal to regain kids' attention. Then invite partners to share their thoughts about the refreshments. Say: **After they escaped from the Egyptians, the Israelites wandered in the wilderness for over a month with nothing to eat but the unleavened bread and water they'd brought with them from Egypt. They were getting tired of it, and they started to complain. Let's find out what they said.**

Distribute Bibles and have kids look up Exodus 16:1-3. When everyone has found the passage, ask a volunteer to read it.

Say: **OK, Israelites. You've had your daily matzo ration. Let's hear your complaints.**

Let kids complain for about 30 seconds, then give the signal to regain their attention. Ask:

● **What would it be like for you to live on unleavened bread and water for weeks?** (Terrible; I'd be tired of eating the same thing; I'd start looking for nuts and berries.)

● **How would you feel about your parents if you were hungry and they didn't find you more food?** (Mad; frustrated; I'd go next door and ask for some food.)

Say: **The Israelites were getting hungry. They were upset at Moses, and they were upset at God. But God was still faithful to them. Let's see how God provided for his people.**

Ask several volunteers to read Exodus

16:4-8, 13-18. Then set out the cooked pie-crust strips and chicken wings.

Say: **This food isn't really manna and quail. But it could be very similar to it in taste. We don't really know what manna tasted like, but we do know that God was faithful to send the manna and quail every day. God wanted the Israelites to understand that he'd meet all their needs. Let's look at another way God met his people's needs.**

THOU SHALT...

(up to 30 minutes)

JIGSAW

p. 7

Read Exodus 19:1-9. Say: **When Moses went up to Mt. Sinai, God gave him the laws that he wanted the Israelites to keep. We know these laws as the Ten Commandments. Today, we're going to look more deeply at these commandments to see what they mean for us today.**

In their family groups, have kids number off from one to four. Have all the ones go to one corner of the room, the twos to another corner, the threes to a third corner, and the fours to the last corner.

Say: **In your corner, you'll find a handout with a Scripture passage and some questions. You'll have about 15 minutes to read the passage and discuss the questions, then you'll return and teach your family members what you learned.**

After about 15 minutes, give the signal to let kids know it's time for them to return to their family groups. Announce that

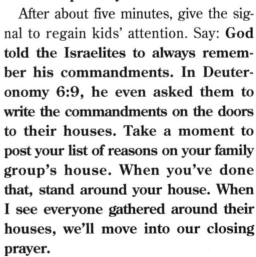

ROAD SIGN Circulate among the corners to monitor kids' progress. To help boost participation, you may want to assign roles. Have groups each choose a recorder to write down their responses, a checker to make sure the group stays on task, a timekeeper to make sure the group finishes on time, and an encourager to make sure everyone participates in the discussion.

the ones will teach first, then the twos, followed by the threes, and then the fours. Allow no more than three to four minutes per teacher.

Invite several kids to share ways they'll keep their commandments this week. Then say: **The Ten Commandments are God's rules for his people. The Israelites were God's people long ago, and we're God's people today. So remember to keep God's commandments this week.**

TEN REASONS

(up to 10 minutes)

LEARNING GROUP

p. 7

Give each family group paper, pencils, and tape. Say: **Now that we've learned what the Ten Commandments are, let's spend a few minutes thinking about why God gave them to us. Work with the people in your family group to list the reasons God gave us each of the Ten Commandments. For example, you might think God gave us the commandment not to lie so people could trust each other. Try to think of at least one reason for each commandment. You'll have about five minutes to come up with your list.**

After about five minutes, give the signal to regain kids' attention. Say: **God told the Israelites to always remember his commandments. In Deuteronomy 6:9, he even asked them to write the commandments on the doors to their houses. Take a moment to post your list of reasons on your family group's house. When you've done that, stand around your house. When I see everyone gathered around their houses, we'll move into our closing prayer.**

THANK YOU, GOD

(up to 5 minutes)

Have families each join hands around their houses, then lead kids in a prayer of thanks for the Ten Commandments. Say: **Let's thank God for his Ten Commandments now. After I say, "We're glad you gave them to us because," I'd like each family to fill in a reason from its list. We'll start with the family closest to me and go around the room to the right.**

Pray: **Thank you, God, for your Ten Commandments. We're glad you gave them to us because...**

Have families take turns filling in reasons from their lists. Keep going around the room until each family has contributed several reasons. Then continue: **Lord,** ▼ **we're your people, and we want to keep your commandments. Listen to our silent prayers as we ask you to help us keep your commandments this week.**

Pause for a moment to allow kids to pray silently, then close by saying: **We love you, God. In Jesus' name, amen.**

Thank kids for coming to class, then congratulate them for working so well together. Pass out the teamwork awards you filled out earlier and encourage kids to post them on their houses or on a bulletin board.

Remind kids to leave their tunics in the classroom and invite them to return next week for the last part of your Exodus journey.

TEN COMMANDMENTS TODAY

Read Exodus 20:1-6. Then work with the people in your corner to answer the following questions about each commandment in your passage. Be prepared to discuss your answers with your family group.

1. How is this commandment kept today?

2. How is it broken today?

3. What happens when this commandment is broken?

4. Name one way you can obey this commandment this week.

Read Exodus 20:7-12. Then work with the people in your corner to answer the following questions about each commandment in your passage. Be prepared to discuss your answers with your family group.

1. How is this commandment kept today?

2. How is it broken today?

3. What happens when this commandment is broken?

4. Name one way you can obey this commandment this week.

Read Exodus 20:13-14. Then work with the people in your corner to answer the following questions about each commandment in your passage. Be prepared to discuss your answers with your family group.

1. How is this commandment kept today?

2. How is it broken today?

3. What happens when this commandment is broken?

4. Name one way you can obey this commandment this week.

Read Exodus 20:15-17. Then work with the people in your corner to answer the following questions about each commandment in your passage. Be prepared to discuss your answers with your family group.

1. How is this commandment kept today?

2. How is it broken today?

3. What happens when this commandment is broken?

4. Name one way you can obey this commandment this week.

LIFE AND DEATH

EXODUS 17-32

- Kids will learn that God is faithful.
- Kids will learn teamwork.

You'll need photocopies of the "Life Points" handout (p. 60), the "Situation Cards" handout (pp. 61-63), and the "Journey to Canaan" game board (pp. 64-65). You'll also need Bibles, the envelopes with the "spoils" cards each family chose during week three of this journey, and a spinner or die.

This entire class is a Bible learning game. Photocopy the "Situation Cards" handout, then cut the cards apart and mix them up. Photocopy the "Life Points" handout and cut out the Life Point cards. You'll need four life points for each family group, plus eight additional cards to give away when kids draw situation cards that entitle them to a free life point. You'll also need to photocopy the game board. If your photocopier has enlargement capabilities, you may want to enlarge the game board.

ROAD SIGN

If you want an extra-large game board, mark a path around your room with sheets of construction paper. Make poster board or newsprint signs to mark the locations of Egypt, the Red Sea, the wilderness, Mt. Sinai, and the Promised Land.

THE JOURNEY: Day 5

JOURNEY TO CANAAN

(up to 45 minutes)

When kids arrive, have them get with their family groups and put on their tunics. Show kids the teamwork cross chart. Review the "sounds like" side and the "looks like" side. Point out positive examples of teamwork you noticed in previous parts of the journey. Then remind them that you'll be looking for positive ways they work as a team with their family groups. Explain that today they can practice teamwork by working together to make decisions as you play Journey to Canaan.

Give groups each a Bible, the spoils cards they chose during the third week of your Exodus journey, and four life points. Set out the game board and the situation cards.

Have groups each quickly choose a playing piece, such as a coin or a piece of chalk, then gather around the game board.

Say: **Our Journey to Canaan game will help us see what it might have been like for the Israelites to wander in the wilderness for many years. We'll learn about some of the other rules God gave the Israelites and discover what happened when those rules were followed or broken.**

As we play, each family group will be a team. After your team draws a card, you must confer together before you decide what to do. Listen carefully as I read the rules for our game.

Read the game rules listed below, one at a time. Be sure to answer any questions kids might have about the rules.

Play the game according to the rules. After you finish, collect the cards, game board, and playing pieces and put them away.

ROAD SIGN
Upper-elementary students are often very concerned about rules and fairness. You may want to photocopy and cut out the game rules and post them near the game board. Kids can then refer to the rules themselves if any disputes come up.

GAME RULES

1. Each team gets six spoils cards and four life points.

2. Figure your team's age by adding up months and years. The oldest team goes first, then play continues clockwise.

3. Roll the die (or spin the spinner) to move on the game board. Each time you land in a space, you must draw a situation card and do what it says. Return your situation card to the bottom of the pile when you're done.

4. If a situation card gives you choices, decide with your team what you should do. If your team doesn't have the supplies to do what the card says, you must skip your next turn.

5. If you draw a "free life point" card, keep it. You'll need it later! If you have to give up a life point, you must give it to the teacher. Don't return it to the pile of situation cards. If your team loses all its life points, you're out of the game.

6. Your goal is to reach Canaan, the Promised Land. Teams who lose all their life points before they reach Canaan must watch the other teams play. The game ends when every team has either lost all its life points or reached the Promised Land.

PROMISES

(up to 15 minutes)

Have kids each find a partner from another family group and discuss the following questions. Pause after you ask each question to allow time for kids to discuss it. Ask:

● **What did you learn from this game?** (The Israelites had a lot of rules; if you got into trouble, you lost your life; some people didn't make it to the Promised Land.)

● **In our game, you had to give up life points or supplies if you broke God's rules. What happens if we break God's rules today?** (Nothing; we get in trouble; we go to jail; it makes God mad.)

Give the signal to regain kids' attention. Invite pairs to share the responses they discussed. Then say: **The Israelites had an agreement with God. If they followed his commandments and trusted his faithfulness, they'd reach the Promised Land. We have an agreement with God, too. If we trust God and do what he wants us to do, God will reward us. Let's close our Exodus journey by discovering God's promises for us.**

Assign each family group a Scripture passage from the following list. If you have a large class, assign the same passage to more than one group. If you have a small class, pick the passages you like the best.

John 3:16
John 14:18-21
Romans 6:23
Romans 8:28
2 Corinthians 4:8-10
Ephesians 1:5-6
Colossians 3:12
Hebrews 8:8b-12
1 John 1:9

After groups have all found their passages, have them discuss the following questions:

● **What does this verse promise?**

● **What does that promise mean in your life?**

Allow a few minutes for kids to read and discuss their passages, then give the signal to bring groups back together. Have groups each choose a representative to read their passages aloud. Say: **Listen quietly, with an attitude of worship, as we hear all that God has done for us.**

Have groups read their passages aloud, one at a time. Then close with a prayer similar to this one: **Dear God, we're thankful to be your people. Thank you for loving us and for sending Jesus to die for our sins. We love you, Lord. In Jesus' name, amen.**

Let kids take their tunics home as a reminder of this journey. Encourage any kids who want to know more about God's promises to talk to you after class.

LIFE POINTS

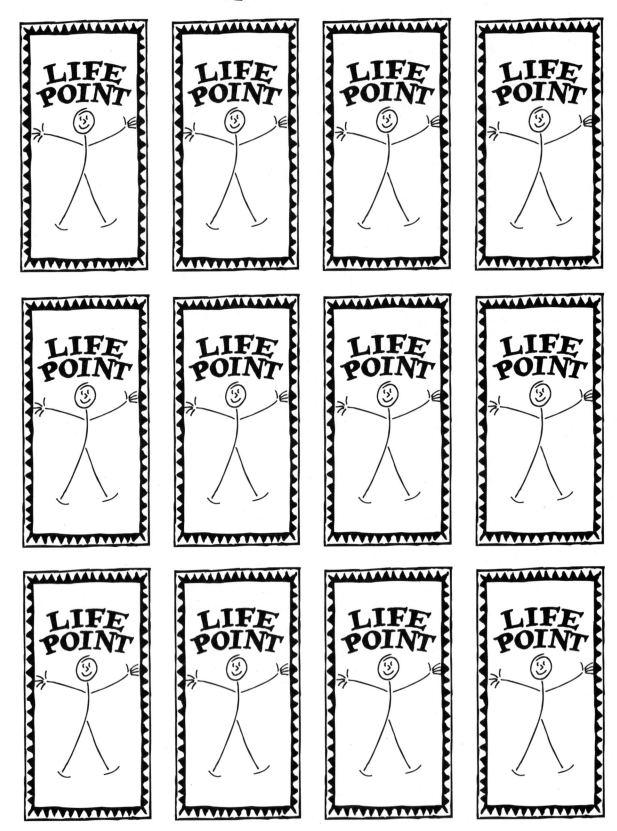

SITUATION CARDS

SITUATION CARD

God is faithful! God has met your needs. Move forward five spaces.

SITUATION CARD

God is faithful! God has met your needs. Move forward five spaces.

SITUATION CARD

God is faithful! God has met your needs. Move forward five spaces.

SITUATION CARD

God is faithful! God has met your needs. Move forward five spaces.

SITUATION CARD

God is faithful! God has met your needs. Move forward five spaces.

SITUATION CARD

God is faithful! God has met your needs. Move forward five spaces.

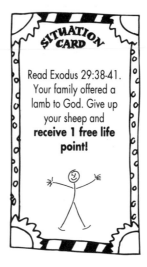

SITUATION CARD

Read Exodus 29:38-41. Your family offered a lamb to God. Give up your sheep and **receive 1 free life point!**

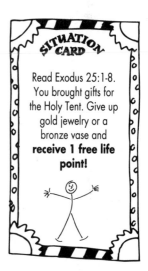

SITUATION CARD

Read Exodus 25:1-8. You brought gifts for the Holy Tent. Give up gold jewelry or a bronze vase and **receive 1 free life point!**

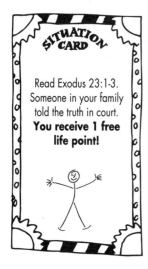

SITUATION CARD

Read Exodus 23:1-3. Someone in your family told the truth in court. **You receive 1 free life point!**

SITUATION CARD

Read Exodus 17:12-13. The men of your family helped move the rock under Moses' arm. **You receive 1 free life point!**

SITUATION CARD

Read Exodus 22:22-24. Your family has been kind to widows and orphans. **You receive 1 free life point!**

SITUATION CARD

Read Exodus 23:10-12. Your family left food in your fields for poor people in the seventh year. **You receive 1 free life point!**

SITUATION CARDS
continued

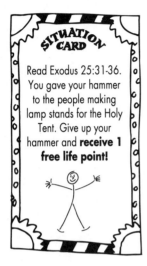

SITUATION CARD

Read Exodus 25:31-36. You gave your hammer to the people making lamp stands for the Holy Tent. Give up your hammer and **receive 1 free life point!**

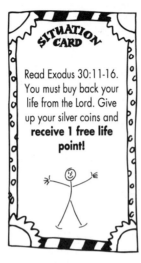

SITUATION CARD

Read Exodus 30:11-16. You must buy back your life from the Lord. Give up your silver coins and **receive 1 free life point!**

SITUATION CARD

A wheel breaks on your cart. You'll need a new wheel.

SITUATION CARD

Your cart is stuck in a ravine. You'll need an ox to pull it out.

SITUATION CARD

A wheel is about to break on your cart. You can fix it with a hammer and some wooden pins.

SITUATION CARD

A windstorm blew your tent away. You need cloth to make a new tent.

SITUATION CARD

Read Exodus 17:8-9. The Amalekites stole two of your supplies. Choose which two supplies to forfeit. Give the forfeited supplies to your teacher.

SITUATION CARD

Read Exodus 32:1-4, 25-29. Two of your family members refused to follow God after worshiping the golden calf. The Levites destroyed them with swords. **Lose 2 life points.**

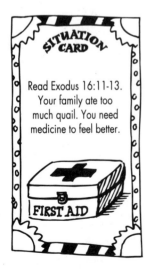

SITUATION CARD

Read Exodus 16:11-13. Your family ate too much quail. You need medicine to feel better.

SITUATION CARD

Read Exodus 17:8-14. One of your family members was killed in the war with the Amalekites. **You lose 1 life point.**

SITUATION CARD

One of your family members was bitten by a snake. You need medicine for your family member to live or you'll **lose 1 life point.**

SITUATION CARD

Read Exodus 19:12-13. One of your family members touched Mt. Sinai and must be stoned to death. **Lose 1 life point.**

SITUATION CARDS

continued

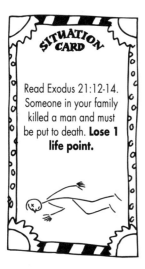

SITUATION CARD

Read Exodus 21:12-14. Someone in your family killed a man and must be put to death. **Lose 1 life point.**

SITUATION CARD

Someone in your family is lost. You must have a ram's horn to help your lost family member find the way back.

SITUATION CARD

Read Exodus 17:8-14. In the battle with the Amalekites, a huge hole was torn in your tent. You need sewing tools to fix it.

SITUATION CARD

Read Exodus 21:12. One of your family members quarreled with another family member and killed him. Your family member must now pay with his or her own life. **Lose 1 life point.**

SITUATION CARD

Read Exodus 21:15. One of your family members attacked your mother and must be put to death. **Lose 1 life point.**

SITUATION CARD

Read Exodus 21:17. One of your family members cursed your father and must be put to death. **Lose 1 life point.**

SITUATION CARD

Read Exodus 21:28. Your bull gored a man. It must be stoned to death and its meat thrown away. **Lose one supply card.** Give the card to your teacher.

SITUATION CARD

Read Exodus 21:29-30. Your bull has a habit of goring people. It has killed a man in the family to your right. That family can demand two supplies or 1 life point.

SITUATION CARD

Read Exodus 21:33-34. You dug a pit and didn't cover it up. The second family on your right had an ox that fell into it. That family can demand one supply from you.

SITUATION CARD

Read Exodus 22:4. Someone in your family stole an ox from the family on your left. You must return the ox and one supply to that family.

SITUATION CARD

Read Exodus 22:20. One of your family members worshiped an idol and must be put to death. **Lose 1 life point.**

SITUATION CARD

Read Exodus 32:33-35. Two of your family members worshiped the golden calf and refused to follow God. A plague will kill both family members. **Lose 2 life points.**

WILDERNESS

MOUNT SINAI

RED SEA

PLACE SITUATION CARDS HERE

JOURNEY WITH DANIEL

"Daniel's God is the living God; he lives forever."
DANIEL 6:26B

After the Babylonians captured Jerusalem, King Nebuchadnezzar took a group of young Israelite men back to Babylon to serve in his palace. He wanted the best and the brightest—the most handsome, intelligent, important young men around. He got the fit and the faithful. Although they were surrounded by Babylonian religious and cultural customs, four men stood firm in their faith. Daniel and his friends resisted the pressure to eat unclean food, and God honored their obedience by giving them great wisdom.

Nebuchadnezzar was impressed by this wisdom, and he gave Daniel and his friends important positions in Babylon. But Daniel, Shadrach, Meshach, and Abednego weren't interested in pleasing the king. More than anything, they wanted to please God. When they were forced to choose between pleasing God and pleasing the king, all four men confidently chose to please God. Even scorching flames and roaring lions didn't sway their resolve. They obeyed God to the end, and God was faithful to deliver them.

In this four-week journey, kids will follow Daniel through the maze of peer pressure. They'll examine the characters of Daniel, the king, and Daniel's accusers. They'll talk about conflicts that arise in pressure situations. Then, as they re-enact Daniel's dramatic encounter with the lions, they'll discover ways God rewards obedience today.

Upper-elementary students are just beginning to experience serious peer pressure. Kids at school may urge them to use drugs or alcohol, cheat on an assignment, or disobey a parent's instructions. Daniel experienced peer pressure most of his life—and successfully resisted it. This journey will draw from Daniel's life to teach kids important lessons about peer pressure. They'll understand the dangers of succumbing to negative peer pressure and the rewards of resisting it. Armed with this knowledge, they'll be ready when their times of testing come.

Try one or more of the following ideas to transform your room into a lions' den:

● Darken the room by covering the windows.

● Play a recording of lion sounds. Recorded sound effects can be checked out from most public libraries.

● Draw faces with sinister or scheming expressions to represent Daniel's accusers. Tape them around the walls as though they're waiting for Daniel to be devoured by the lions.

● Place skeleton-like bones in the corners of the room—remains of a previous feast.

PRESSURE PIT

DANIEL 6

● Kids will learn that God honors obedience.
● Kids will learn encouragement.

You'll need photocopies of the "Christlike Character-Quality Observation Chart" (p. 9), Bibles, newsprint, tape, and a marker.

● Don't forget to select a signal!

ROAD SIGN

If you've used other journeys in this book, you may want to vary the "Prepare With Prayer" introduction. But keep in mind that you may have new students who haven't heard the information before. If you do vary the introduction, don't forget to start with prayer!

THE JOURNEY: Day 1

PREPARE WITH PRAYER

(up to 5 minutes)

Say: **Today marks the start of an exciting adventure for our class. We're going to be learning about events that happened long ago in Bible times. But we're not just going to read or talk about them; we're going to create a Bible-times environment right here in our classroom and experience Bible events as if we were actually there. It will be like taking a journey back to Bible times.**

Ask:

● **When have you taken a journey?** (When I went to my grandma's for Thanksgiving; when our family went on vacation; when my scout troop went camping.)

● **What was your favorite part of the journey?** (Flying in an airplane; coming home to my friends; seeing my cousins.)

● **What new things did you discover on the journey?** (I learned how to put up a tent; I saw a bald eagle; I went to three states I'd never been to before.)

Say: **Journeys are a lot of fun. We get to be with our family or friends, and we get to do fun things and see new places. Sometimes we learn new things when we go on journeys. During our journey back to Bible times, we'll be learning new things about God and about each other. We'll have to work together and help each other along the way. Let's ask God to help us do that.**

Pray: **Dear God, thanks for giving us the Bible to help us learn about you. Please be with us as we go on our journey. Help us work together as we learn new things. In Jesus' name, amen.**

DESTINATION: ENCOURAGEMENT

(up to 5 minutes)

Say: **Our Bible journey is going to take us back to the time of Daniel. We'll learn how Daniel obeyed God even when it was hard and how God delivered Daniel from the lions' den. As we go on our journey together, we'll also be learning encouragement. What do you know about encouragement?** (Let kids respond.)

Say: **Encouragement means supporting others and helping them to have confidence. If you've ever experienced applause after a big game or recital, you know about encouragement. When parents or friends come to watch our activities, we feel loved and supported.**

Ask:

● **What other examples of encouragement can you think of?** (Going to my sister's band concert; calling a friend who's feeling depressed; cheering for my brother's soccer team.)

● **Why is it important to encourage others?** (It makes people feel good; someday you might need someone to encourage you; it helps people do their best.)

Say: **As we go on our journey together, be thinking of ways you can show encouragement. To help us remember about encouragement, let's** make a chart.

Post a sheet of newsprint and draw a cross chart as described on page 8. Write "encouragement" above the cross.

Say: **We're making this chart in the shape of a cross to remind us that Jesus encouraged others, too. When the disciples were sad or afraid, Jesus encouraged them. After Jesus went back to heaven, he sent the Holy Spirit so we'd never be without encouragement. As Christians, we always have the Holy Spirit as our special, personal encourager.**

On the left side of the cross, let's write what encouragement sounds like. What kinds of things would you hear people say if they're showing encouragement?

List kids' responses on the newsprint. They may say that encouragement sounds like "Great job," "You're really good at that," or "How can I help you?"

Say: **On the right side of the cross, let's write what encouragement looks like. What kinds of things would you see people doing if they're showing encouragement?**

List kids responses on the newsprint. They may say that encouragement looks like kids helping each other, giving each other hugs or pats on the back, or praying for each other.

Say: **You can use this chart to help you remember to practice encouragement. I'll be looking at our chart, too, and watching for people or groups who are showing encouragement.**

WARM-UPS

(up to 10 minutes)

Say: **We're going to have a drama** ▼ workshop today. We'll practice several different methods of acting. Then over the next three weeks, we'll create a Bible drama to present to our families and friends.

The first method of acting we'll try is dramatic sculpture. But first we need to stretch and warm up our muscles.

Have kids stand up, stretch, and shake their arms and legs to loosen up. Then lead them in doing 20 jumping jacks.

ROAD SIGN To make this activity even livelier, play kids' favorite contemporary Christian music in the background.

After the exercises, say: **OK, actors and actresses, let's get started. In dramatic sculpture, you'll shape your body into various objects. I'll call out the objects, and then you'll use your legs, arms, upper body, and head to make the shape of that object. Let's practice that. We'll start out with a cactus.**

Shape yourself into a cactus and encourage kids to do the same. Then say: **That's pretty good. Now let's try a more advanced technique. Let's make cactuses again—but this time with partners. Find a partner near you and create a cactus shape using both of your bodies.**

After pairs have formed their cactus shapes, say: **Great! Let's try another one. Find three people and create a sewing machine.**

After kids have formed their sewing machines, have them try sculptures from the following list:

● Statue of Liberty (whole class)

● a giraffe (groups of two or three)

ROAD SIGN It's OK to have several groups of three and one group of two or four. Encourage kids to work together no matter what their group size.

- a banana (one person)
- a tomato (groups of four or five)
- a table (groups of three or four)
- a box (groups of two, three, or four)
- a tree (one person)
- a lion (whole class)

Say: **Those were great sculptures. We may need some human tables or trees when we do our Bible drama. And we'll definitely need some lions. Let's read the story we'll be working on and find out what else we might need.**

EXPRESSIONS

(up to 15 minutes)

p. 7

Have kids form trios and number off from one to three. Give each trio a Bible and have kids look up Daniel 6 and be ready to follow along as the story is read. Say: **Our Bible story focuses on the characters of King Darius, Daniel, and Daniel's accusers. We can learn a lot about characters by studying their feelings and expressions. As I read the story, I'll assign each person to be one of the characters. Think about how your character might be feeling in that situation. When I stop reading, make a face that shows how your character might be feeling. Don't say anything—just make a face. The ones will be King Darius, the twos will be Daniel, and the threes will be Daniel's accusers.**

Read Daniel 6:1-4, then have kids make their faces. Repeat the process for each of the following passages. Each time, have kids make faces to demonstrate their characters' feelings.

- Daniel 6:5-9
- Daniel 6:10

- Daniel 6:11-14
- Daniel 6:15-18
- Daniel 6:19-22
- Daniel 6:23-24
- Daniel 6:25-28

After you read the last passage, say: **I saw some very interesting faces. Now let's talk about the feelings behind some of those expressions. I'll ask you a few questions, and you'll answer from your character's point of view.**

Ask trios the following questions. Pause after you ask each question to allow time for kids to discuss it. Ask:

- **How did your character feel when Daniel was given an important position?**
- **How did your character feel when Daniel was caught praying?**
- **How did your character feel when Daniel was thrown in the lions' den?**
- **How did your character feel when God saved Daniel?**

After kids have discussed the last question, give the signal to regain their attention. Invite kids to share the feelings they discussed in their trios. List the feelings on a sheet of newsprint. Then say: **All the characters in this story showed strong feelings. Daniel's accusers were angry and jealous. King Darius was proud of his power, then sad about punishing Daniel, and then happy when Daniel was saved. Daniel was determined to follow God. He may have been scared when he was thrown in the lions' den, but he knew God would protect him. If we follow God, God will protect us just as he protected Daniel.**

ROAD SIGN Save the newsprint list of characters' feelings. You'll need it next week when you start planning your drama.

IMPROV THEATER

(up to 20 minutes)

Have kids remain in their trios. Say: **Daniel had a tough choice to make. He could follow the king's law and keep his important position, or he could follow God and face the lions' den. If you were in Daniel's place, what would you do?** (Stop praying; make sure I didn't get discovered; trust God to save me like Daniel did.)

Continue: **I hope none of us will ever face a den of hungry lions. But we sometimes face other people or situations where it's hard to follow God. We're going to look at one of those situations as we continue our drama workshop with some improvisational theater. In improvisational theater, you don't have already-written lines to read. Instead, you start with some characters and a setting, and then you make up the lines and the action as you go along.**

I'll give you the characters and the setting, and then I'll describe the situation. After I finish, you'll confer with your trio and decide what the characters should do in that situation. Then you'll make up some lines to finish the story and present it to the class. Everyone in your trio must be involved in the drama you present.

The characters in this situation are Taylor; Taylor's best friend, Jamie; and Jamie's older brother, Jeremy. Taylor is a Christian. Jamie isn't a Christian but has gone to church with Taylor a few times. Taylor and Jamie are in fifth grade. Jeremy is in college.

When Jeremy came home from college for the summer, he offered to buy Jamie some wine. Jamie invited Taylor over and told Taylor about Jeremy's offer. "Wouldn't that be awesome?" Jamie said. "We could give some to all our friends, and they'd think we were really cool! Our parents would never know." Taylor wasn't so sure. Their parents were pretty smart. But even if their parents didn't find out, Taylor didn't think it was right. Jamie called Taylor a chicken and threatened to tell all their other friends that Taylor was afraid to try some wine. **What does Taylor do?**

Allow several minutes for trios to discuss the situation and come up with a short drama. Then have trios take turns presenting their dramas. Applaud each trio and affirm them for a job well done. After the last drama has been presented, ask kids the following questions:

● **How is Taylor and Jamie's situation like Daniel's? How is it different?** (They both had to make a tough choice; Taylor and Jamie's situation could really happen today; they both had bad consequences.)

● **When have you been in a situation like this?** (When my friend wanted to copy my homework; when some older kids started selling drugs behind our school; when kids at school made fun of

> **ROAD SIGN**
> The characters of Taylor and Jamie could be boys or girls. If you have some trios that are all girls, let them change Jamie's older brother to an older sister. If boys or girls don't want to be Taylor or Jamie, they can change the names.

> **ROAD SIGN**
> As trios work together, use a photocopy of the "Christlike Character-Quality Observation Chart" (p. 9) to monitor how well they're practicing encouragement. Use a separate observation chart for each trio. Be positive with your comments but be sure to note one or two areas where trios could be more encouraging.

me for going to church.)

● **How did you handle it?** (I asked God to help me; I walked away; I looked for some new friends.)

Say: **God honored Daniel's obedience, and he honors our obedience, too. The Bible tells us that if we trust God, he'll help us do what's right. Let's close by letting God know how we feel about him.**

SCULPTED PRAYERS
(up to 5 minutes)

Say: **For our closing prayer, let's do one last dramatic sculpture. Let's sculpt our bodies into prayers to God. If you feel thankful, you might bow** ▼ **your head in gratitude. Or, if you feel appreciative, you might pretend to applaud for God. I'll give you one minute to determine what you'll do. When I use the signal, sculpt yourself into that prayer and freeze in that position until I say "amen."**

Give the signal and let kids make their sculptures. After one minute of posing, say "amen."

Give trios each a "Christlike Character-Quality Observation Chart." Have them discuss ways they can better encourage one another next week. Encourage kids to return next week when you'll be shaping and writing your Daniel drama.

PLAYWRIGHT

DANIEL 6

- Kids will learn that God honors obedience.
- Kids will learn encouragement.

You'll need photocopies of the "Christlike Character-Quality Observation Chart" (p. 9), newsprint, a marker, tape, paper, pencils, and Bibles. Use the Packing Tips below and kids' presentation ideas to determine any additional supplies you may need.

You may want to recruit three or four adults to help kids plan their presentation. Assign one adult volunteer to each presentation group. Stress to the adults that they'll be serving as resources for the kids. Rather than running the groups, they'll be helping kids carry out their own ideas. If you have volunteers who are artists, carpenters, writers, or seamstresses, pair them up with appropriate presentation groups.

Gather resources kids can use as they plan their presentation. Choose from the following list, or add your own creative resources.

- Look through your church's children's-music collection for songs about Daniel. If your church doesn't have much music on hand, you may want to call around to other churches in your area or take a trip to your local Christian bookstore. If possible, obtain recordings of any songs you find. If you can't find recordings, ask a member of your church choir to come in and sing the songs for the kids.

- Gather children's Bibles and books about Daniel. Try to find a few with pictures. Encourage kids to read several versions of the story to get ideas for the script, sets, and costumes.

- Provide tempera paints, newsprint, poster board, and other art supplies for kids to create scenery.

- If your church has a collection of Bible-times costumes, bring them to class. If not, collect old, adult-sized T-shirts or children's bathrobes for costumes.

- Provide lamps and flashlights for the sound and light group. Check your local library for recorded sound effects. Kids will especially enjoy the sound of lions roaring.

● If you think your presentation might include a music video, bring in contemporary Christian music that deals with temptation or peer pressure, such as "Be Strong and Courageous" or "The Race Is On," by Michael W. Smith, or "Walk On By," by Susan Ashton. Ask teenagers in your church for other music ideas.

THE JOURNEY: Day 2

DRAMA SHAPING

(up to 10 minutes)

Before class, write each of the following questions on a separate sheet of newsprint. Post the newsprint sheets side by side on a wall.

1. What kind of presentation should we have?
2. From whose point of view should it be told?
3. What should the tone of our presentation be?
4. What kind of costumes will we need?
5. What should the set or scenery look like?
6. What shall we call our presentation?

When children arrive, have them sit in a circle. Say: **We have a lot to accomplish today as we plan to present the story of Daniel in the lions' den. First, we'll work together to make some decisions about our Daniel drama. Then we'll work in groups to create the script, costumes, sets, and special effects for our drama. I've posted some questions to help us get started. We'll discuss them one at a time.**

Choose someone to be the recorder for the first question, then lead kids in brainstorming ideas about what kind of presentation they'd like to do. If kids need help getting started, suggest things such as pantomime, dance, music video, drama, or a modern-day version of Daniel's story.

> **ROAD SIGN**
> If new kids have joined your class this week, you may want to re-read the story of Daniel in the lions' den from Daniel 6 before you begin brainstorming.

After you finish discussing the first question, narrow the answers to the choice or choices the entire group can agree on. Then choose a new recorder and discuss the second question. Remind kids that the story could be presented from any character's point of view, from a narrator's point of view, or from their point of view.

> **ROAD SIGN**
> Remember that there are no wrong answers in brainstorming! Use any outrageous responses to spark other ideas. Have your recorder list all ideas for each question.

Move on to questions 3 through 5. After you finish discussing each question, narrow the answers, then choose a new recorder. When you talk about costumes and scenery, make sure kids consider all the different characters and settings they want to include.

After you've finished discussing tone, costumes, and scenery, choose a new recorder and begin taking suggestions for a title. Narrow the list to three or four titles. You may want to choose the final title by secret ballot vote. Kids could put their heads down and raise their hands, or they could each write their choices on a piece of paper.

Announce the final title, then say: **Our Daniel presentation is starting to take shape. We've got some good ideas for costumes, sets, and scenery. Now it's time to put those ideas in motion.**

PLAY PLANNERS

(up to 35 minutes)

p. 7

Form four groups and give each group paper and pencils. Have the first group write the script and/or choose the music for the presentation; the second group design and create the set; the third group plan the costumes; and the fourth group create special effects, such as sounds and lighting. Encourage groups to reread Daniel 6 if they have any questions as they work.

Say: **As you work, plan for everyone to be involved in the final production—even if some people work behind the scenes. You'll need to talk to other groups as you work to make sure the entire production will work well together.**

Work closely with each group to offer ideas and help them determine what part each child will play in the presentation. Encourage kids to use any supplies they can find in the classroom, as well as the additional resources ▼

ROAD SIGN
As groups work together, use a photocopy of the "Christlike Character-Quality Observation Chart" (p. 9) to monitor how well each group is practicing encouragement. Use a separate observation chart for each group. Be positive with your comments but be sure to note one or two areas where groups can improve their encouragement. Hold on to these charts until the end of class.

you've brought. If groups need additional supplies, encourage kids to collect things themselves. If kids do need help gathering supplies, remind them to let you know today so you can collect things before next week.

Watch the clock as kids are working. When you have about 15 minutes left in class, give the signal. Wait for kids to respond, then say: **Collect your supplies and gather in the center of the room. When everyone has gathered, we'll report on our progress.**

REPORTS

(up to 15 minutes)

Have groups report what they've each planned for their part of the presentation. Ask if they need any help and note any supplies you'll need to collect this week. Say: **Our Daniel drama is taking shape. Let's pray and ask God to guide our work as we close our class today. Dear God, thank you for the story of Daniel. As we study his life in preparation for our drama, help us remember his example. Be with us when we face tough situations, just as you were with Daniel in the lions' den. Help us to follow you this week. In Jesus' name, amen.**

Collect any scripts, notes, costumes, or sets and put them in a safe place in your classroom until next week. Give groups their "Christlike Character-Quality Observation Charts." Have them discuss ways they can better encourage one another next week. Encourage kids to return next week, when you'll put your presentation together and begin rehearsals.

PRACTICE 'TIL PERFECT

DANIEL 6

- Kids will learn that God honors obedience.
- Kids will learn encouragement.

You'll need any additional supplies children requested last week. You'll also need markers; pencils; and photocopies of the parent's letter (p. 81), the "Christlike-Character Awards" handout (pp. 11-13), the "How's It Going?" handout (p. 10), and the lion invitation art (p. 80).

Photocopy the parent's letter and fill in the title, date, and times of your presentation. (Children should arrive at least 30 minutes before you plan to start the program.) Be sure to sign each letter. You'll need one letter for each child in your class.

Photocopy the "Christlike-Character Awards" handout onto colored paper. You'll need at least one encouragement award for each presentation group. Cut off the other award sections from each handout and save them for use in other journeys.

Make one photocopy of the "How's It Going?" handout for each group.

Photocopy the lion invitation art. Make several for each child. Ask several adult volunteers to help you with the dress rehearsal.

ROAD SIGN

Remind kids to practice encouragement in today's class. As they work, complete and distribute an encouragement award (p. 13) to each group.

THE JOURNEY: Day 3

LEARNING GROUP

p. 7

FINAL PREP

(up to 15 minutes)

As kids arrive, have them find their groups and work to finish up their preparations for the presentation. If you have new kids, have them join the sets and scenery group. After 15 minutes, use your signal to let kids know their time is up.

Collect the script from the script group and have one of your volunteers photocopy it while kids evaluate their encouragement in the next activity. Kids should each have their own photocopies, whether or not they have speaking parts.

CRITIC'S CHOICE

(up to 5 minutes)

Say: **As we begin rehearsing for our presentation, you'll need to work closely with the people in your group to make sure your part of the presentation goes smoothly. Your group will also need to work with other groups to bring all your contributions together into one presentation. We'll need a lot of encouragement for our presentation to succeed. So before we start practicing, let's pause for a few minutes and think about how our encouragement is going.**

Give each group a "How's It Going?" handout (p. 10) and a pencil. Have the kids in each group fill out the handout together as they discuss

ROAD SIGN Circulate between groups as they're discussing their progress. Be an example of encouragement as you help groups work on problems that may arise. If some groups just aren't working well together, help them think of specific actions to get along better. Encourage groups that are working well together to think of ways they can make their groups even better.

how their group is doing.

After all groups have finished their evaluations, collect the handouts and have groups gather in the center of the room. Say: **Now we're ready to start our rehearsal. Let's ask God to bless our practice time. I'd like you to spend a minute or two praying for the group on your right. Then I'll close.**

After a minute or two, close with a prayer similar to this one: **Dear God, thank you for our friends in this class. Help us to honor you by encouraging others and by our presentation of Daniel's story. We want to trust you like Daniel did. In Jesus' name, amen.**

After your prayer, say: (Name of your presentation), **take 1!**

DRESS REHEARSAL

(up to 30 minutes)

Distribute photocopies of the script and help the script group explain each part of the presentation. Make kids all understand their parts. Have kids take their places—whether they'll be playing parts onstage or working sets, scenery, or special effects behind the scenes. Run through the presentation as many times as you can so kids are comfortable with their parts.

ROAD SIGN If you need more time for practice, put off the formal presentation to families and friends for one more week. Rehearse again in class next week or set up another time for an extra rehearsal.

YOU'RE INVITED

(up to 10 minutes)

Have kids each find a partner from a different presentation group. Set out markers and the photocopied lion invitation

PAIR SHARE

p. 6

art. Say: **Work with your partner to make invitations to our presentation. You can take turns lettering the invitations, coloring the pictures, and adding borders or other special touches. Make sure you include the title, time, and place of the presentation on each invitation.**

Let kids work on their invitations until the end of class time. Point out that they can write in the large lion's mouth or on its mane. Encourage them to take their invitations home to give to family members and friends. Before kids leave, tell them what time they should arrive for next week's presentation. Give each child a photocopy of the parent's letter on page 81.

DEAR PARENT,

For the past three weeks, our class has been on a Bible journey with Daniel. We've learned important lessons about trusting God even in tough situations. As a part of our Daniel journey, we've been preparing a dramatic presentation. It's called

_____,

and we'll be presenting it to parents and friends on

_____.

The presentation begins at _____,

and children should arrive at _____.

Please bring a plate of finger foods to share.

We look forward to seeing you!

Sincerely,

SHOWTIME

DANIEL 6

DESTINATION

● Kids will learn that God honors obedience.
● Kids will learn encouragement.

For each child, you'll need a photocopy of the "Outstanding!" award (p. 84) and a single long-stemmed rose. If you can, purchase white, yellow, or red roses. Boys may not like pink or purple!

You'll also need a video camera, a television, a VCR, and party decorations.

GEAR

PACKING TIPS

Make photocopies of the "Outstanding!" award and fill in kids' names. If you have a calligraphy pen, use it to add a formal touch to the notes.

Set up tables in a fellowship hall or other large meeting room for the finger foods your audience will bring. Decorate the room for a party.

Arrange for someone in your congregation to videotape kids' presentation. Set up a television and VCR so you can watch the tape immediately after the presentation.

> **ROAD SIGN**
>
> The times given for activities in this session are approximate and may vary depending on the type of presentation your class has chosen. If you're limited to a one-hour time period, plan to show the video of your production another time.

THE JOURNEY: Day 4

BACKSTAGE

(up to 30 minutes)

When kids arrive, have them put on their costumes. Have adult volunteers ready to help kids set up the sets, scenery, and lighting. When you're almost ready to begin, give the signal and have kids gather backstage or in a nearby room. Ask one of the kids to pray for your production, then have them all take their places for the show.

WELCOME

(up to 5 minutes)

Walk to the front of the audience and give the signal you've been using in class. Say: **Welcome! The signal I just used is the same one we've been using in our class. The kids have been working in small groups on different parts of the production, and we use that signal to let each other know when it's time to stop working and move on to the next activity. Our next activity today is to present** (name of your presentation). **But before we start, I wanted to tell you what a great time we've had getting this production ready for you.** (Name of your presentation) **is the result of lots of great individual and team effort! We hope you enjoy the show.**

CURTAINS!

(up to 30 minutes)

Have children present their program.

APPLAUSE! APPLAUSE!

(up to 10 minutes)

After the program, have the entire cast take a bow together. Then have each presentation group step forward and take a bow. After the audience's applause dies down, have kids sit on the stage or on the floor in front of the audience. Say: **We couldn't have put on this presentation without the help of each person in our class. We've all worked hard, and along the way we've learned to trust God and each other. Right now, I'd like to give each cast member a special award.** (To kids) **I hope this award will remind you of Daniel's example and encourage you to trust God this week and every week.**

As you read each child's name, present him or her with a single rose and an "Outstanding!" award. After you've given out all the awards, lead the audience in a final round of applause.

CAST PARTY

(up to 45 minutes)

Invite families and friends to enjoy the finger foods and visit with the cast members. If you're planning to show the video of the performance immediately, set it up while people go through the snack line. Kids will enjoy watching themselves perform immediately after their presentation.

Outstanding!

You stand up for Jesus. And you stand out among the crowd!

Child's Name

Copyright © Christine Yount. Published in *Extra-Special Bible Adventures for Children's Ministry* by Group Publishing, Inc., Box 481, Loveland, CO 80539.

JOURNEY WITH JESUS

"Jesus answered, 'I am the way, and the truth, and the life.'"
JOHN 14:6A

Kids today believe in so many heroes. Movie heroes like Batman and Indiana Jones capture their imaginations. Sports figures like Michael Jordan loom larger than life. At school, they learn about important religious and political leaders like Mohammed, Buddha, and Nelson Mandela. How many more heroes do they need? And where does Jesus fit in? Is he a popular religious leader like Mohammed? Is he a superhero with amazing powers?

The Christian faith rises and falls on the person of Jesus Christ. In Jesus, God himself came down to earth to redeem his beloved creation from sin. He took on human flesh and dwelt among us, and while he was here, he changed the world. Jesus healed sick people, freed captives, and comforted the broken-hearted. He touched lepers, he hugged children, and he changed lives. His death and resurrection stand as proof that Jesus truly is the Son of God.

During this four-week journey, kids will encounter Jesus as the people of his day encountered him. They'll hear from John the Baptist, Lazarus, Mary Magdalene, and the thief on the cross. They'll discover how Jesus fulfilled Old Testament prophecy. They'll learn all they can about Jesus' time on earth, and then they'll perform an earthly ministry of their own.

Kids today are growing up in a culture where everything is relative. To many of their school teachers and friends, Christianity is simply one choice among many. The kids in your class need to know the absolute truth about Jesus Christ. This journey will teach kids that Jesus is God's promised Savior and will give them an opportunity to make Jesus a part of their lives.

Depending on the size of your room, you may want to do some or all of the following things to give your room the feel of a village in Jesus' day:

● Set up a canopy or tent to use as your meeting area.

● Create the "Sea of Galilee" by laying a blue blanket or sheet in a corner of your room. Set a small boat on the blanket to make it look like it's floating on the sea. You can even add paper fish and a fishing net off one side of the boat.

● Draw New Testament-style houses. Cut out the houses and put them up in your room.

● Open cans of tuna or sardines to make your room smell like a real village by the sea.

● Provide a Bible-costumes box with robes, sheets, or ready-made tunics for kids to wear during this journey. You can find instructions for making tunics in the Exodus journey on page 35.

● If your church or another church nearby puts on an outdoor nativity scene, see if you can borrow some life-size animals. Don't forget to set out hay so they won't get hungry!

PROMISE FULFILLED

1 CORINTHIANS 15:3-4

- Kids will learn that Jesus is God's promised Savior.
- Kids will learn kindness.

You'll need newsprint; a marker; tape; a deck of playing cards; a photocopy of the "John the Baptist Monologue" script (p. 91); and photocopies of the "Old News" (p. 92), "Good News" (p. 93), and "In My Name" handouts (p. 94). You'll also need photocopies of the parent's letter on page 95. Be sure you sign each letter.

- Don't forget to choose a signal!
- Ask an adult or teenage male in your church to play the part of John the Baptist. Give your actor a photocopy of the "John the Baptist Monologue" script and have him study the lines and prepare his costume. Have your actor arrive early.
- Make enough photocopies of the "Old News" handout for one half your class and enough photocopies of the "Good News" handout for the other half.
- Look over the "In My Name" handout. Think of people in your church or community who kids could possibly perform ministries for. Be prepared to share these names with children today.

ROAD SIGN If you've used other journeys in this book, you may want to vary the "Prepare With Prayer" introduction. But keep in mind that you may have new students who haven't heard the information before. If you do vary the introduction, don't forget to start out with prayer!

THE JOURNEY: Day 1

PREPARE WITH PRAYER

(up to 5 minutes)

Say: **Today marks the start of an exciting adventure for our class. We're going to be learning about events that happened long ago in Bible times. But we're not just going to read or talk about them; we're going to create a Bible-times environment right here in our classroom and experience Bible events as if we were actually there. It will be like taking a journey back to Bible times.**

Ask:

● **When have you taken a journey?** (When I went to my grandma's for Thanksgiving; when our family went on vacation; when my scout troop went camping.)

● **What was your favorite part of the journey?** (Flying in an airplane; coming home to my friends; seeing my cousins.)

● **What new things did you discover on the journey?** (I learned how to put up a tent; I saw a bald eagle; I went to three states I'd never been to before.)

Say: **Journeys are a lot of fun. We get to be with our family or friends, and we get to do fun things and see new places. Sometimes we learn new things when we go on journeys. During our journey back to Bible times, we'll be learning new things about God and about each other. We'll have to work together and help each other along the way. Let's ask God to help us do that.**

Pray: **Dear God, thanks for giving us the Bible to help us learn about you. Please be with us as we go on our journey. Help us work together as we learn new things. In Jesus' name, amen.**

DESTINATION: KINDNESS

(up to 5 minutes)

Say: **Our Bible journey is going to take us back to the time of Jesus. We'll meet some people who knew Jesus, and we'll work together to perform ministries of service for people in our church or community. As we go on our journey together, we'll also be learning kindness. What do you know about kindness?** (Let kids respond.)

Say: **Kindness means treating others with respect and gentleness. No matter how big or small or mean or friendly people are, God wants us to treat them kindly. When you play ball with your little brother or sister, you're showing kindness. When you get up early to fix a special breakfast for your mom or dad, that's kindness, too. Ephesians 4:32 tells us to be kind and forgiving to each other because God has forgiven us.**

Ask:

● **What other examples of kindness can you think of?** (Helping a friend with a homework assignment; baking cookies for a neighbor; offering to baby-sit for free.)

● **Why is kindness important?** (It makes people feel good; God wants us to be kind; if you're kind to other people, they'll be kind to you.)

Say: **As we go on our journey together, be thinking of ways you can show kindness. To help us remember about kindness, let's make a chart.**

Post a sheet of newsprint and draw a cross chart as described on page 8. Write "kindness" above the cross.

Say: **We're making this chart in the shape of a cross to remind us that Jesus showed kindness, too. When Jesus was here on earth, he showed kindness to children, families, old people, sick people—everyone he met. What examples of kindness can you think of from Jesus' life?** (When Jesus healed people; when he fed the 5,000; when he died for us.)

Say: **On the left side of our cross, let's write what kindness sounds like. What kinds of things would you hear people say if they're showing kindness?**

List kids' responses on the newsprint. They may say that kindness sounds like "That's OK; try again" or "Could you please hand me the scissors?"

Say: **On the right side of our cross, let's write what kindness looks like. What actions would you see people doing if they're showing kindness?**

List kids' responses on the newsprint. They may say it looks like a pat on the back, soft eyes, or a smile.

Say: **As we go on our journey, you can use this chart to help you remember to practice kindness. I'll be looking at our chart, too, and watching for people or groups who are showing kindness.**

ROAD SIGN

Have your "John the Baptist" stand outside the door and listen as you prepare your kindness cross chart. When he hears you tell kids that you'll be looking at the cross chart, too, have him burst into the room.

REPENT!

(up to 10 minutes)

Without any introduction, have your John the Baptist enter the room, present his drama, and leave abruptly. (See the "John the Baptist Monologue" script on page 91.)

After John the Baptist leaves, ask:

● **What do you think that message meant?** (Get ready for Jesus to come; stop doing bad things.)

● **How would you have felt if you'd heard the real John the Baptist preach?** (Scared; confused; ready to repent; wondering why he was so weird.)

● **Why do you think God sent John the Baptist before Jesus?** (So people would be ready for Jesus; to baptize people; to make people repent.)

Say: **God planned to send John the Baptist long before John was actually born. Way back in Old Testament times, God used prophets to tell people what he was going to do before he did it. The prophet Isaiah predicted that someone would come and help people get ready for Jesus. John the Baptist fulfilled Isaiah's prophecy.**

The Bible contains many prophecies about Jesus, too. Old Testament prophets predicted that God would send a Savior. When Jesus came, he fulfilled their predictions. Let's learn about some prophecies about Jesus now.

FULFILLED

(up to 15 minutes)

Form pairs. Have kids in each pair choose to be either an "oldie" or a "newie." Then have the oldies go to one side of the

JIGSAW

ROAD SIGN The pairs you form in this activity will stay together for the "Ministry Pairs" activity. Because partners will be required to work together on a ministry project outside of class, it's best to pair up children who are friends or who live near each other.

room and the newies go to the other side. Distribute photocopies of the "Old News" handout (p. 92) to the oldies and photocopies of the "Good News" handout (p. 93) to the newies. Choose a reader and a discussion leader for each group. If you have a large class, you may want to have the oldies and newies each form several smaller groups. Choose a reader and a discussion leader for each small group.

Say: **Read your handout and discuss the questions. In a few minutes, you'll return to your original partner and tell that person what you learned.**

After seven or eight minutes, have kids return to their partners. Have partners work together to match up the Old Testament prophecies about Jesus with the New Testament fulfillments of prophecy.

After pairs have matched up all the prophecies, say: **Jesus fulfilled all the Old Testament prophecies about himself. Let's find out what that means for our faith.**

JUST BY CHANCE?

(up to 10 minutes)

PAIR SHARE
p. 6

Give a deck of playing cards to a child. Have the child shuffle the cards and give them back to you. Have children help you lay out the cards on the floor, face down. Ask a volunteer to select the ace of hearts.

Kids may say this is impossible and refuse to try it. If someone volunteers, give that person one

ROAD SIGN If your church is uncomfortable using playing cards, use the cards from an Old Maid, Go Fish, Memory, or Concentration game. Lay out the cards the same way, choosing another card to use instead of the ace of hearts.

chance to find the card, then ask the following questions. If no one volunteers, have kids tell you why they won't try to find the card, then continue with the questions below.

Have kids find their partners from the previous activity to discuss the following questions. Pause after you ask each question to allow time for kids to discuss it. Ask:

● **What are the chances of our volunteer finding the ace of hearts on the first try?** (No chance; impossible unless the volunteer cheated; good only if the volunteer was really lucky.)

● **Prophets in the Old Testament predicted Jesus' coming. Jesus fulfilled every one of their prophecies. What are the chances of an impostor fulfilling all the Old Testament prophecies about Jesus?** (Like our chances of picking the ace of hearts; not very likely; impossible.)

● **What does Jesus' fulfillment of every Old Testament prophecy tell us about Jesus?** (That he's for real; God was planning to send Jesus for a long time; the prophets knew a lot about Jesus even though he hadn't come yet.)

● **How would your faith be different if Jesus hadn't fulfilled the prophecies about himself?** (I'd think he was a fake; I wouldn't have faith in him if he weren't real.)

After kids have discussed the last question, give the signal to regain their attention. Invite several pairs to share the responses they discussed. Then say: **If Jesus hadn't fulfilled the Old Testament prophecies, we wouldn't know for sure that he's God's Son. But he did fulfill the prophecies. He was born** in Bethlehem, he spent his time on earth helping people, and he went on to die for our sins. Jesus is God's promised Savior and our example for living out our Christian faith. Let's find out ways we can follow Jesus' example this week.

MINISTRY PAIRS

(up to 10 minutes)

PAIR SHARE

p. 6

Give each partner a photocopy of the "In My Name" handout (p. 94). Say: **Your partner is now your ministry partner. For the next three weeks, you'll work with your partner outside of class to perform a ministry of service like Jesus did. Use the "In My Name" handout to help you think of a ministry you can do. I'll be available to give you names of people in our church or community who need help. You have 10 minutes to come up with a ministry idea.**

Walk around the room and answer any questions kids may have. Pairs may choose to do the same kind of ministries, but they must carry out their ministries separately. After 10 minutes, give the

signal and have kids gather to report on their ministries.

COMMISSIONED

(up to 5 minutes)

Have pairs report on the ministries they've chosen. If some kids are having trouble choosing a ministry, ask them to check with you after the closing prayer for help. After everyone has given his or her report, close with a prayer similar to this one: **Dear God, thanks for sending Jesus. He's our Savior and our example. Bless us as we follow Jesus by ministering to people in need during the next few weeks. In Jesus' name, amen.**

Have kids write their names on their handouts and circle the ministries they've chosen. Collect the handouts so you'll have a record of the ministries kids are planning to do. Give kids each a photocopy of the parent's letter on page 95 and have them fill in their ministry partners' names and the ministries they've chosen. Encourage them to return next week when you'll learn about Jesus' power.

JOHN THE BAPTIST MONOLOGUE

To the actor:

Familiarize yourself with this monologue by reading it several times. You don't need to memorize it—but whatever you do, don't "read" it! Follow the suggestions below to present a convincing John the Baptist through your words, costume, gestures, and "stage presence."

Costume:

Use a burlap sack to make yourself a tunic. In the top of the sack, cut a hole big enough for your head to fit through. Cut an armhole on each side of the sack. Wear a pair of shorts under the tunic.

You'll want to look like a wild man! Try using mousse or hair spray to scruff up your hair or a dark eyebrow pencil to smear "dirt" on your face, arms, and legs.

Character tips:

John the Baptist was like a wild man. As you present your monologue, pace around the room and wave your arms in the air. Lean over every now and then to get very close to a child's face as you speak. Once your monologue is finished, leave the room as abruptly as you entered.

SCRIPT

(As you enter the room abruptly, cry out:) **Repent! Repent! Turn from your sins, for the kingdom of God is coming!**

(Continue with the following lines:)

I am John the Baptist—a mere voice crying in the wilderness!

Prepare the way for the Lord!

Do you think I am someone great? I am not! I am just a servant preparing the way for the great one!

He is more powerful than I. And I am not even fit to carry his shoes.

I baptize with water, but he will baptize with power and the Holy Spirit.

Repent! Repent!

The Lord is near! The kingdom of God is at hand! Repent!

OLD NEWS

Read all of the following Scriptures. For each Scripture you read, discuss these questions:

- Who are these verses talking about?
- What do these verses tell us about this person?
- Does this person sound like someone you'd like to know? Explain.

" 'The Lord himself will give you a sign: The virgin will be pregnant. She will have a son, and she will name him Immanuel' " (Isaiah 7:14).

"This is the voice of one who calls out: 'Prepare in the desert the way for the Lord. Make a straight road in the dry lands for our God' " (Isaiah 40:3).

"He was hated and rejected by people. He had much pain and suffering. People would

not even look at him. He was hated, and we didn't even notice him" (Isaiah 53:3).

"But he was wounded for the wrong we did; he was crushed for the evil we did. The punishment, which made us well, was given to him, and we are healed because of his wounds" (Isaiah 53:5).

"The Lord God has put his Spirit in me, because the Lord has appointed me to tell the good news to the poor. He has sent me to comfort those whose hearts are broken" (Isaiah 61:1a).

"But you, Bethlehem Ephrathah, though you are too small to be among the army groups from Judah, from you will come one who will rule Israel for me. He comes from very old times, from days long ago" (Micah 5:2).

Good News

Read all of the following Scriptures. For each Scripture you read, discuss these questions:

- Who are these verses talking about?
- What do these verses tell us about this person?
- Does this person sound like someone you'd like to know? Explain.

"So Joseph left Nazareth, a town in Galilee, and went to the town of Bethlehem in Judea, known as the town of David. Joseph went there because he was from the family of David. Joseph registered with Mary, to whom he was engaged and who was now pregnant. While they were in Bethlehem, the time came for Mary to have the baby, and she gave birth to her first son. Because there were no rooms left in the inn, she wrapped the baby with pieces of cloth and laid him in a box where animals are fed" (Luke 2:4-7).

"During Elizabeth's sixth month of pregnancy, God sent the angel Gabriel to Nazareth, a town in Galilee, to a virgin. She was engaged to marry a man named Joseph from the family of David. Her name was Mary. The angel came to her and said, 'Greetings! The Lord has blessed you and is with you.' But Mary was very startled by what the angel said and wondered what this greeting might mean. The angel said to her, 'Don't be afraid, Mary; God has shown you his grace. Listen! You will become pregnant and give birth to a son, and you will name him Jesus' " (Luke 1:26-31).

"At this time, the word of God came to John son of Zechariah in the desert. He went all over the area around the Jordan River preaching a baptism of changed hearts and lives for the forgiveness of sins. As it is written in the book of Isaiah the prophet: 'This is a voice of one who calls out in the desert: "Prepare the way for the Lord. Make the road straight for him. Every valley should be filled in, and every mountain and hill should be made flat. Roads with turns should be made straight, and rough roads should be made smooth. And all people will know about the salvation of God!" ' " (Luke 3:2b-6).

" 'The Lord has put his Spirit in me, because he appointed me to tell the Good News to the poor. He has sent me to tell the captives they are free and to tell the blind that they can see again. God sent me to free those who have been treated unfairly and to announce the time when the Lord will show his kindness' " (Luke 4:18-19).

"He came to the world that was his own, but his own people did not accept him" (John 1:11).

"But God shows his great love for us in this way: Christ died for us while we were still sinners" (Romans 5:8).

Copyright © Christine Yount. Published in *Extra-Special Bible Adventures for Children's Ministry* by Group Publishing, Inc., Box 481, Loveland, CO 80539.

In My Name

Jesus said that anything we do for even the least of his people, we also do for him. Use the list below to help you think of a ministry you can perform to help others. Choose an idea from this list or use these ideas to think of other ministries:

✝ Bake cookies for a shut-in and deliver them.

✝ Write secret notes of encouragement to 10 people in your church and mail them.

✝ Take a care package to someone in the hospital or a nursing home.

✝ Do a job, such as mowing a lawn or cleaning someone's house, to raise money. Then use that money to help someone else; for example, buy school supplies or new clothes for another child.

✝ Mow someone's yard for free.

✝ Call 10 different people and tell them that Jesus loves them.

✝ Set up a lemonade stand and give the lemonade away.

✝ Be a servant for the day. Volunteer to help someone in your church and do whatever that person wants for one day.

✝ Go through your closets. Send some of your clothes and toys to an orphanage or children's home in your area. (Ask your parents for permission first.)

✝ Send a care package to a college student or someone in the armed services who's away from home.

✝ Volunteer to help out a mom with young kids by playing with her children at her house one afternoon.

✝ Send a care package to a missionary family your church sponsors. Send packages of nonperishable items that don't weigh very much, such as Jell-O, muffin mix, or pizza mix.

✝ Volunteer to help out in the church nursery. Plan activities you can do with the little children, such as puppet shows or simple crafts.

DEAR PARENT,

For the next three weeks, our class will be on a Bible journey with Jesus. We'll meet Bible characters who knew Jesus and learn how Jesus is God's promised Savior. As part of our Jesus journey, kids will be performing ministries of service as Jesus did. Your child's ministry partner is _____.

Their ministry will be _____

_____.

We encourage you to get involved in your child's ministry. You can help by offering to provide transportation or supplies or simply by supporting and praying for your child.

We're excited about this opportunity to serve others in our church and community!

Sincerely,

DYNAMITE POWER

JOHN 11:25

DESTINATION

- Kids will learn that Jesus is God's promised Savior.
- Kids will learn kindness.

You'll need chalk and a chalkboard or a marker and newsprint, paper, pencils, Bibles, scissors, one photocopy of the "Character List" handout (p. 100), one photocopy of the "Lazarus Monologue" (p. 99), and several photocopies of the "Christlike Character-Quality Observation Charts" (p. 9).

GEAR

PACKING TIPS

● Photocopy and cut apart the "Character List" handout. Kids will be working in groups of four, and each group will receive a section of the handout. You'll need a different Bible character for each child in your class, so if you have more than six groups of four, you may need to research a few additional characters.

● Ask an adult or teenage male in your church to play the part of Lazarus. Give your actor the "Lazarus Monologue" script and have him prepare his costume and script. Have "Lazarus" arrive early to take his place in a corner of your room. Tell him not to move until it's time to present his monologue.

> **ROAD SIGN**
> Kids will probably notice Lazarus sitting in the corner. If they ask you about him, simply shrug your shoulders. Tell kids that he's been sitting there for a while and they should probably leave him alone.

THE JOURNEY: Day 2

KINDNESS REVIEW

(up to 5 minutes)

Show kids the kindness cross chart they made last week. Review the "sounds like" side and the "looks like" side. Ask kids if they'd like to add anything to either side. Then remind them that you'll be looking for positive ways they show kindness to others during class today.

PAIR SHARE
p. 6

MINISTRY PROGRESS

(up to 10 minutes)

Have kids get with their ministry partners and discuss how their ministries are going. Ask pairs if they're having any problems. If so, encourage other pairs to give ideas to solve the problems. Celebrate any success stories kids have to share.

LEARNING GROUP
p. 7

CHARACTER ROLES

(up to 30 minutes)

Form groups of four. If you have an uneven number of kids, it's OK to form a group of three or five. Write the following questions on newsprint or a chalkboard for kids to use as they study their characters.

ROAD SIGN
As groups work together, use a photocopy of the "Christlike Character-Quality Observation Chart" (p. 9) to monitor how well they're practicing kindness. Use a separate observation chart for each group. Specifically, observe the items on the cross chart. Be positive with your comments but be sure to note one or two areas where groups can show more kindness. Hold on to these charts until the end of class.

● Who is this person?
● What does the Bible tell us about this person?
● How did this person know Jesus?

Distribute paper, pencils, and Bibles to each group. Then give each group a list of four biblical characters from the "Character List" handout (p. 100). Tell kids not to show or tell their characters to other groups. Keep a list of the characters you distribute to each group to use during the fourth week of this journey.

Say: **I've given each group a list of four Bible characters. Do not reveal the names of your characters to other groups. In your group, work together to choose a character for each person. Each person must have a different character.**

ROAD SIGN
If you have a group of five, assign that group an additional character. Make sure you haven't assigned this character to any other group! It's important for each child to choose a different character.

After you've each chosen a character, study that character on your own to learn as much as you can about him or her. Use the questions posted on the newsprint and the Scripture verses on your character list to help you. Make notes of things you learn. We'll have more time to study our characters next week. Right now, you'll have 30 minutes.

After about 30 minutes, quietly signal your Lazarus to begin his monologue.

ALIVE!

(up to 10 minutes)

Without any introduction, have Lazarus awaken and present his drama. (See the "Lazarus Monologue" script on page 99.) After the monologue, have Lazarus leave the room.

After Lazarus leaves, ask:
● **How did you feel when Lazarus came to life in our room?** (Scared;

weird; funny.)

● **How do you think the real Lazarus' family and friends felt when he came to life?** (Excited; confused; happy; thankful to have him back.)

● **What does Jesus' raising Lazarus from the dead tell us about Jesus' being God's promised Savior?** (He really is God's promised Savior; only God could have that much power; someday Jesus will raise us from the dead and take us to heaven.)

● **When Jesus raised Lazarus from the dead, he used the power God had given him to help one of his followers. How can Jesus' power help you in your life today?** (Help me remember to pray; heal my grandpa's cancer; make my mom and dad stop fighting.)

Say: **Jesus is God's promised Savior. He was the only person powerful enough to raise Lazarus from the dead. And Jesus uses that same power to help us every day. He has power to comfort us when we're sad, heal us when we're sick, and free us when we're trapped by temptation. Let's close our class by thanking God for that power and asking him to put it to work in our lives this week.**

CORNER PRAYERS

(up to 5 minutes)

CORNERS

p. 6

Have children stand in the center of the room. Say: **We all need God's power. We're going to ask God for his power in different areas. I'll ask you a question and then give you some possible responses. When you hear me mention the person or area you want to pray for, go to the corner of the room I point out. When everyone**

is in a corner, I'll lead us in a prayer.

As you give responses to each question, point to a different corner. Allow children time to walk to that corner. After everyone is in a corner, lead the prayer.

Ask: **Who do you know that needs Jesus' power? A family member. A friend. A classmate. Someone in our church.**

Pray: **Dear God, please use your power to help the people we love and care about.**

Ask: **Where do you need Jesus' powerful help in your life? In a friendship. At school. At home. In some other area.**

Pray: **Dear God, we need your powerful help to be strong in these areas. Please help us.**

Ask: **What's one problem in the world that you'd like to see God's power make a difference in? Crime and violence. Hunger. Homelessness. Drug abuse.**

Pray: **God, our world is broken, and we need you to fix it. Please send your power to our world.**

After the last corner prayer, have kids all return to the center of the room and join hands. Pray: **God, we know you have great power. Thank you for sending your power to help us. Thank you for changing our lives. In Jesus' name, amen.**

Before kids leave, give each group its "Christlike Character-Quality Observation Chart." Have groups each choose one way to work on kindness based on your observations. Encourage kids to return next week when you'll learn about Jesus' forgiveness.

LAZARUS MONOLOGUE

To the actor:

Familiarize yourself with this monologue by reading it several times. You don't need to memorize it—but whatever you do, don't "read" it! Follow the suggestions below to present a convincing Lazarus through your words, costume, gestures, and "stage presence."

Costume:

Use strips torn from a white bedsheet to wrap yourself up, mummy style. If you can't get a bedsheet, you can use several rolls of bathroom tissue. You may want to get someone to help with this! Wrap the strips loosely around your knees, elbows, and hips to allow for bending. Cover your face completely, but allow openings so you can see and breathe.

SCRIPT

(At the appropriate time in the lesson, begin moaning and groaning. Move slowly as though you're just awakening. Stand and present your monologue.)

Oh! My aching bones!

It's not easy to be dead, you know.

(Stretch.) Oh! That feels good!

That tomb can really do a number on your back.

Do you know who I am? My name is Lazarus. I'm a friend of Jesus'. And what a friend he turned out to be!

When I first got sick, I was mad at Jesus because he wouldn't come and heal me. My sisters sent for him, you know, but he wouldn't come. And I thought he loved me.

Well, needless to say, my sisters were really mad. I hate to say this, but we all kind of doubted that Jesus even had the power to make me well. I'm ashamed now to say that.

Hey, by the way, why don't some of you help me get these grave clothes off. Sorry about the stench.

(Have kids help unwrap you.)

That's better.

Anyway, where was I? Oh, yeah! Jesus came to my grave after I had died. Talk about power! All he had to do was say, "Lazarus, come forth." And I came back to life. I'll never doubt his power again!

Cʜᴀʀᴀᴄᴛᴇʀ Lɪsᴛ

Directions: Photocopy this handout and cut apart the lists of characters. Give a different set of characters to each group. Do not allow groups to hear or see the characters you give to other groups.

Peter—John 1:35-51; John 13; John 18:1-27; John 20:1-10; John 21:1-19
Judas Iscariot—Matthew 26:1-5, 14-25, 47-56; Matthew 27:1-10
Pilate—Matthew 27:1-2, 11-31; Mark 15:1-20; Luke 13:1-9; Luke 23:1-25; John 18:28–19:16
Caiaphas—Matthew 26:1-5, 57-68; Luke 3:1-2; John 11:45-57; John 18:12-24; Acts 4:1-12

John the Baptist—Luke 1:5-25, 57-80; Luke 3:1-22
Andrew—Matthew 4:17-22; Luke 9:1-6; John 1:35-50; John 6:1-15; John 12:20-26; Acts 1:6-14
James—Matthew 4:21-22; Matthew 17:1-9; Luke 9:1-6; Mark 10:35-45
John—Matthew 17:1-9; Luke 9:1-6; Mark 1:29-31; Mark 10:35-45

Philip—Matthew 10:1-8; Luke 9:1-6; John 1:40-51; John 6:1-15; Acts 8:26-40
Matthew—Matthew 9:9-13; Luke 6:14-15; Luke 9:1-6
Thomas—Luke 9:1-6; John 11:1-16; John 20:24-29
Zacchaeus—Luke 19:1-10

Roman soldier—Luke 7:1-10
Mary (Jesus' mother)—Matthew 1:16-25; Luke 1:26-56; Luke 2:1-21; John 19:25-27; Acts 1:14
Bartimaeus—Mark 10:46-52
Boy with the lunch—John 6:1-15

Roman soldiers—John 19:16-24
Woman at the well—John 4:1-42
Martha—Luke 10:38-42; John 11:1-44
Leper—Luke 5:12-16

Paralytic—Mark 2:1-17
Woman whose son was brought to life—Luke 7:11-17
Girl raised from the dead—Luke 8:40-56
Rich young ruler—Mark 10:17-31

Copyright © Christine Yount. Published in *Extra-Special Bible Adventures for Children's Ministry* by Group Publishing, Inc., Box 481, Loveland, CO 80539.

FORGIVEN

1 JOHN 1:7-9

- Kids will learn that Jesus is God's promised Savior.
- Kids will learn kindness.

You'll need chalk and a chalkboard or a marker and newsprint, masking tape, paper, Bibles, one photocopy of the "Mary Magdalene Monologue" script (p. 105), and several photocopies of the "Missing the Mark" handout (p. 106).

- Ask an adult or teenage female in your church to play the part of Mary Magdalene. Give your actress a photocopy of the "Mary Magdalene Monologue" script and have her prepare her costume and script. Have "Mary Magdalene" arrive early.

THE JOURNEY: Day 3

CROSS-CHART CHECK

(up to 5 minutes)

Show kids the kindness cross chart they made the first week. Review the "sounds like" side and the "looks like" side. Ask kids if they'd like to add anything to either side. Point out kindnesses you've seen in previous parts of the journey. Then remind kids that you'll be looking for positive ways they show kindness to others during class today.

MINISTRY PROGRESS

(up to 5 minutes)

PAIR SHARE
p. 6

Have kids get with their ministry partners and discuss how their ministries are going. Remind kids that they need to complete their ministries by next week. Encourage ministry pairs to pray for God's blessing on their ministries.

CHARACTER QUESTIONS

(up to 20 minutes)

LEARNING GROUP
p. 7

Have kids return to their character-list groups from last week. Encourage individuals to complete any additional Bible study they need to learn about their characters.

Write the following questions on a chalkboard or newsprint.

● Who was Jesus Christ?

● What would you say to Jesus if he were here today?

Have kids discuss the questions in their groups. Have each person answer from his or her character's point of view.

If groups finish discussing the questions before you're ready to move on,

have them work on ideas for costumes they could wear to dress up as their characters next week.

After about 15 minutes, give the signal to regain kids' attention. Say: **Without revealing the identity of your character, turn to a partner from another group and answer this question: "How could your character have prevented Jesus from dying on the cross?"**

Let kids discuss the question for about five minutes, then invite them to share their responses. Then say: **We couldn't have done anything to prevent Jesus from dying on the cross. Jesus had to die so we could be forgiven and have eternal life. We've all sinned and done wrong things, and God can't stand sin. But because God loved us and wanted us to have eternal life with him, he sent Jesus to die for our sins. Let's take a closer look at what sin is.**

UNDERSTANDING SIN

(up to 10 minutes)

Using masking tape, create a line down the middle of your room. Designate one end of the line as "agree" and the other end as "disagree." Say: **I'm going to read several statements about sin. After I read each statement, line up on the tape to show whether you agree or disagree with the statement. For exam-**

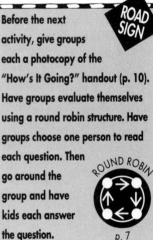

ROAD SIGN

Before the next activity, give groups each a photocopy of the "How's It Going?" handout (p. 10). Have groups evaluate themselves using a round robin structure. Have groups choose one person to read each question. Then go around the group and have kids each answer the question.

ROUND ROBIN
p. 7

LINEUPS
p. 6

ple, if you definitely agree with the statement, you'd stand at the "agree" end of the line. If you definitely disagree, you'd stand at the "disagree" end. If you're not sure, you'd stand somewhere in the middle.

Read the following statements. Pause after you read each statement to give children time to place themselves on the line. After everyone is standing on the line, have kids discuss their stance with the person next to them. Allow a few minutes for discussion, then read aloud the verse in parentheses.

It's a sin just to think about doing something wrong. (James 1:14-15)

Some people never sin. (Romans 3:23)

Some sins are worse than other sins. (1 John 5:17)

Say: **When we do wrong things and break God's rules, that's sin. When we fail to do the good things God wants us to do, that's sin, too. Sometimes we sin with our actions, and sometimes we sin with our thoughts. But all of us sin every day. And the Bible says in Romans 6:23 that the punishment for sin is death. That's why we need Jesus. When Jesus died on the cross, he took the punishment for sin forever. Because of Jesus, we can have God's forgiveness and eternal life!**

CLEANSED

(up to 10 minutes)

Without any introduction, have your Mary Magdalene enter the room, present her drama and then leave. (See the "Mary Magdalene Monologue" script on page 105.)

After the monologue, read aloud Luke ▼

7:36-50. Have kids discuss the following questions with a partner. Pause after you ask each question to allow time for kids to discuss it. Ask:

● **How do you think the people in Simon the Pharisee's house felt when Mary came in and started anointing Jesus' feet?** (Embarrassed; confused; wondering how she got in the house.)

● **Why was Simon upset at Jesus?** (Because he didn't think Mary deserved to touch Jesus; he didn't think Jesus should be around sinners; because Mary wasted the perfume.)

● **Why did Jesus forgive Mary for her sins?** (Because she anointed his feet; because she loved him; Jesus forgives everyone's sins.)

● **Are there any sins Jesus can't forgive? Why or why not?** (No, Jesus forgives everyone; I'm not sure if Jesus forgives mass murderers.)

Give the signal to regain kids' attention, then ask partners to share the responses they discussed. Say: **In 1 John 1:9, the Bible tells us that if we confess our sins, God forgives us. It doesn't matter how bad we've been or how rotten we feel. The minute we ask for forgiveness, we've got it. Let's close by playing a game to see what it would be like to live life without God's forgiveness.**

ROAD SIGN

If kids get into a discussion about which sins can be forgiven, ask volunteers to read Matthew 12:31-32. Explain that the Pharisees had spoken against the Holy Spirit by saying that Jesus' power came from Satan instead of from God's Holy Spirit. They deliberately refused to acknowledge that Jesus had power to heal people and to forgive their sins.

Read 1 John 1:9. Explain that God forgives our sins, but we have to ask for his forgiveness. People who permanently turn their backs on God won't be forgiven because they'll never ask for forgiveness. If kids want to know more, or if you feel uncomfortable leading a discussion about sin and forgiveness, consider inviting your pastor to come and answer kids' questions after class or next week.

MISSING THE MARK

(up to 10 minutes)

Tape several photocopies of the "Missing the Mark" handout (p. 106) to the wall. Have kids stand five feet from the wall. Give kids each a sheet of paper and have them wad it up. Then have them turn their backs to the wall, bend down, and throw their paper wads through their legs toward the handout's target.

Kids may have to take turns doing this, but make sure everyone gets to try it at least once. As they're throwing their paper wads, say things such as "Come on—it's not so hard" or "There must be someone in this class who can hit the target."

After everyone has had a chance to throw a paper wad at the target, have kids throw their paper wads in the trash. Then ask:

ROAD SIGN *If your church recycles paper, use sheets of paper that are headed for the recycling bin for this activity!*

● **What was it like to try to hit the target with your paper wad?** (Hard; impossible; I could have done it if you didn't make us throw through our legs.)

● **How is that like or unlike trying to live a perfect life?** (Both are impossible; if I practiced long enough I might hit the target, but I'll never be perfect.)

Say: **It was difficult to hit the target every time. And that's the way it is with sin. It's impossible to be perfect in the sight of God. We're never right on target. Even though we try to be good, we still keep sinning. Sinfulness is part of being human. But even though we're sinful, God still loves us. That's why Jesus had to die. Jesus is God's solution for our sin problem.**

Let's close our class with a special prayer of thanks for God's forgiveness. We'll start by standing along the walls to remind us that without forgiveness, we're far away from God. After I read each sentence, say, "Thank you, Jesus" and take one step toward the center of the room. This will remind us how Jesus' death on the cross brought us forgiveness and let us get close to God. When we all reach the center, we'll form a tight circle and close by saying, "Jesus, we love you" together.

When kids have lined up along the walls, read the following prayer. After you read each line, pause for kids to say, "Thank you, Jesus."

Pray:

Lord, we know we're sinful, but you love us anyway.

Each day we sin, but each day you forgive us.

It's hard for us to forget our sins, but we know you do.

The minute we confess our sins to you, you're faithful to forgive us.

With your forgiveness, our sins are far away, as far as the east is from the west.

When you died on the cross, you took away our sins forever.

Form a circle and close by saying together, "Jesus, we love you. Amen."

Encourage children to come dressed as their Bible characters next week for a Bible masquerade party.

ROAD SIGN *Some children may have more questions about what Jesus' death on the cross means to them. Be prepared to stay after class to answer any questions.*

MARY MAGDALENE MONOLOGUE

To the actor:

Familiarize yourself with this monologue by reading it several times. You don't need to memorize it—but whatever you do, don't "read" it! Follow the suggestions below to present a convincing Mary Magdalene through your words, costume, gestures, and "stage presence."

Costume:

Wear a long skirt or a dress, large earrings, and many bracelets. A shawl would be a nice extra touch. Wear sandals or no shoes. Bring a pitcher of water, a towel, and a small washtub or basin with you. A porcelain or clay pitcher and basin will give the most authentic Bible-times feel.

SCRIPT

(Enter the room carrying the pitcher filled with warm water, the washtub, and a towel. Silently walk to a child and begin to take off his or her shoes. If the child allows this, wash the child's feet as you do the monologue. If the child resists, just sit back on the floor and present your monologue.)

Washing feet is a custom of my time. We don't have paved streets or sidewalks. After a day of going to the market and walking from village to village, our feet get pretty dirty. The dust from the roads gets all over our feet.

Well, it wouldn't be good manners to go into someone's house with dirty feet. So a good host or hostess provides a place for guests to wash their feet when they come into the house.

(Thoughtfully) I once washed the feet of a great man. I had heard of his ministry to people—healing sick people, giving sight to the blind, and giving hearing to the deaf. I wanted to do something for this great man, but I wasn't worthy. There was something so holy about him.

Anyway, I heard this man was in town. So I took my best and most expensive perfume, and I went to the house where he was. No one had washed Jesus' feet. I couldn't believe how rude this host was. So I opened my perfume and began to wash his feet.

He looked at me with such great love in his eyes that I began to weep. My tears flowed down and fell on his feet.

When I was done, I knew that I had touched the feet of God. Only God could show such love and forgiveness to a sinner like me.

MISSING THE MARK

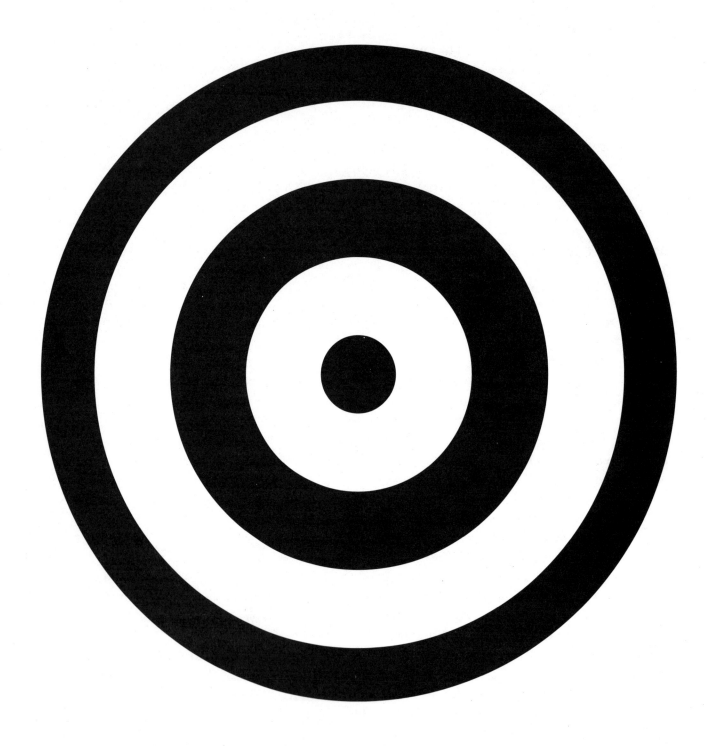

MEET WITH JESUS

JOHN 6:35

● Kids will learn that Jesus is God's promised Savior.
● Kids will learn kindness.

You'll need a kindness award (p. 12) for each child. You'll also need Bible-costume accessories, photocopies of the "Who Am I?" handout (p. 110), a photocopy of the "Thief-on-the-Cross Monologue" script (p. 111), pencils, and French bread.

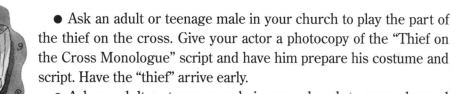

● Ask an adult or teenage male in your church to play the part of the thief on the cross. Give your actor a photocopy of the "Thief on the Cross Monologue" script and have him prepare his costume and script. Have the "thief" arrive early.

● Ask an adult or teenage male in your church to come dressed as Jesus and be prepared to act out the role of Jesus as kids mingle in costume during the "Masquerade Party" section of the lesson. For an extra touch, decorate the room with streamers for a party. Play kids' favorite contemporary Christian music as they're mingling.

● Photocopy the "Who Am I?" handout. You'll need one copy for each child. If you didn't use all the characters, be sure to let kids know who's "missing" at your party.

● Have one of your kids' parents bring a video camera to class today to preserve this masquerade party. Kids will enjoy watching the video later.

● Just before class, pour a cup of grape juice for each child. Set the cups on a table or counter where they'll be out of kids' way. You may want to cover them with a paper towel to keep kids from drinking them during the party.

> **ROAD SIGN**
>
> Kids will come dressed in character today. You can add to the fun by dressing up in biblical costume yourself. Be sure to bring extra clothing for costumes just in case some children forget to dress up.

THE JOURNEY: Day 4

MASQUERADE PARTY

(up to 20 minutes)

As kids arrive, remind them to practice kindness in today's journey. Encourage them to visit with "Jesus" and each other while they're waiting for other kids to arrive. Have "Jesus" greet characters as if he knows them. But make sure he doesn't reveal any character's name.

When everyone has arrived, use the signal to get kids' attention. Give them each a "Who Am I?" handout (p. 110) and a pencil. Say: **We have a room full of famous people here this morning. Each person in our class represents a different Bible character. You all have one thing in common: You know a man named Jesus. As you talk to each other, ask each other questions to figure out who each person represents. You may ask any question except a flat-out "Who are you?" or "What's your name?" When you think you've guessed a character, write the name of the person representing that character on your handout.**

ROAD SIGN As kids are mingling, complete a kindness award for each child. Hold on to these until later.

After about 15 minutes, give the signal to regain kids' attention. Have them gather in the center of the room. Then read down the list of characters and have the student representing each character stand up. Have the person playing Jesus stand up, too. He may leave at this point or stay for the rest of the class. Applaud everyone for their performances.

Say: **We don't get to see Jesus face to face as these people did, but we can still love and follow him. We've learned a lot about Jesus by studying our characters and hearing from people like Lazarus and Mary. We also learn about Jesus by serving other people. Let's find out how our ministries of service turned out.**

GOOD REPORTS

(up to 15 minutes)

Have children get with their ministry partners and sit in a circle. Ask partners to give brief ministry reports. Affirm each pair for the ministry they've accomplished, then present each child with a kindness award. Thank kids for being so kind, like Jesus would be.

After everyone has given a report, give thanks together for all the great ministry God has done through the kids in your class.

FORGIVEN

(up to 10 minutes)

Without any introduction, have your thief on the cross enter the room, present his monologue, and then leave. (See the "Thief-on-the-Cross Monologue" on page 111.)

After the monologue, say: **We have so much to be thankful for. God has been at work through each of us during this journey. We've accomplished some great ministries, and we've learned a lot about Jesus, God's promised Savior. Like the thief on the cross, we can be thankful to God for the forgiveness and eternal life he gives us** through Jesus. Let's take a few minutes to think about that together.

REMEMBER ME

(up to 15 minutes)

Say: **Jesus met the thief when they were both hanging on the cross to die. Just before Jesus went to the cross to die, he shared a meal with his disciples. During that meal, he asked them to remember him. We're going to share a loaf of bread and remember Jesus together now.**

Hold up the loaf of French bread. Say: **We're going to pass this bread around our circle. When it comes to you, break off a piece and then tell us something you'd like to thank God for. You might want to thank God for something specific, like helping you feel better when you were sick. If you can't think of something specific, you can thank God for his forgiveness or for sending Jesus. Hold on to your piece of bread until everyone has been served.**

Pass the bread around the circle. When everyone has been served, have children eat their bread. Say: **Thank you, God, for** ▼

being part of our lives. We especially thank you for sending Jesus to die so we can be forgiven. We remember Jesus now.**

Have the person playing the thief on the cross ask to join the circle. Encourage children to make a place for him. Say: **Like the thief on the cross, we've all sinned and need God's forgiveness. Let's take a moment to pray about that.**

Allow a few moments of silence, then lead children in a forgiveness prayer. Pray: **God, we've all sinned. Thank you for loving us anyway. We're sorry for the wrong things we've done. Please forgive us. In Jesus' name, amen.**

Have children put their arms around each other and tighten the circle. Then close with a prayer similar to this one: **Dear God, thank you for sending us Jesus to be our Savior. We've learned a lot from him about kindness, love, forgiveness, and service. Help us put those things into practice in our lives. Forgive us when we fall short, and make us more like Jesus every day. In his name, amen.**

WHO AM I?

Directions: See how many characters you can guess correctly. Look at the characters on the left side. On the right side, write the name of the person you think is playing that character.

CHARACTER	NAME
Peter	
Judas Iscariot	
Pilate	
Caiaphas	
John the Baptist	
Andrew	
James	
John	
Philip	
Matthew	
Thomas	
Zacchaeus	
Roman soldier	
Mary (Jesus' mother)	
Bartimaeus	
Boy with the lunch	
Roman soldiers	
Woman at the well	
Martha	
Leper	
Paralytic	
Woman whose son was brought to life	
Girl raised from the dead	
Rich young ruler	

Copyright © Christine Yount. Published in *Extra-Special Bible Adventures for Children's Ministry* by Group Publishing, Inc., Box 481, Loveland, CO 80539.

THIEF-ON-THE-CROSS MONOLOGUE

To the actor:

Familiarize yourself with this monologue by reading it several times. You don't need to memorize it—but whatever you do, don't "read" it! Follow the suggestions below to present a convincing thief on the cross through your words, costume, gestures, and "stage presence."

Costume:

No special clothes are needed for this role. A pair of old jeans and a T-shirt will work fine.

SCRIPT

(Walk into the room. Pace as you talk and rub your hands together nervously.)

Hi! You don't know me. I have a name, but you'll never know it. But that's OK. My name isn't important.

What I do for a living is important. I'm a thief. I'm a good thief. I've stolen jewels, money, and food. *(Pretend to hold up and admire a stolen item.)* **Once I stole a precious gem from Caesar's palace. It was gorgeous. But that's when I got caught—and convicted. They sentenced me to the cruelest death possible—death on a cross.**

(Walk to a wall and pantomime as you talk. Pound your feet, then one hand at a time to the wall. Stay on the "cross" until you say, "But I knew I had to pay for what I'd done.")

So they nailed my feet, my hand, and my other hand to the cross. Such agony. But I knew I had to pay for what I'd done.

It didn't seem fair to me that the one they call Jesus was crucified beside me. He had never done anything wrong.

I knew it, and so did the other thief on the cross. But he made fun of Jesus. I stood up for Jesus, and I told the other thief that Jesus was innocent. That's when Jesus said that I would be in paradise with him. I died because of all *I* had done wrong. But Jesus died because of all the things *we* had done wrong.

As he hung on the cross, he looked down through the ages and saw you *(point)* **and you** *(point)* **and you** *(point)***. He saw each one of you.**

Have you figured it out yet? Jesus died for us. Our sins nailed him to the cross. And his love for us kept him there.

(Thoughtfully) **"This day you shall be with me in paradise."**

(Leave the room, then quietly re-enter. After kids eat their bread, ask if you can join the circle.)

JOURNEY WITH PAUL

"After I had this vision from heaven... I began telling people that they should change their hearts and lives and turn to God."
ACTS 26:19-20A

When Paul was named Saul, he persecuted Christians with a vehemence. He hated them. Saul had probably never met the man named Jesus Christ, but he sure didn't like the effect this Jesus was having on the Jews who were following him. Saul put all of his energies into hunting down and killing Christians.

But God had special plans for Saul. As he was traveling to Damascus, Saul encountered Jesus Christ. Saul was radically changed by his experience. From that time on, Saul was a different man, and thus he had a new name—Paul. Paul poured all his passion and energy into proclaiming the power of the Jesus he once sought to destroy. He traveled from city to city to show and tell about God's love through Jesus Christ. Paul's encounter with Jesus guided his every action for the rest of his life.

On this two-day journey, children will gather at the church for a service retreat. They'll enjoy fellowship with one another as they hear Paul's incredible story. They'll act out Paul's escape and shipwreck through Bible learning games. Then they'll go out to serve the community just as Paul did.

Kids today want to help make the world a better place. Every day on the news, they see images of children wounded by war and ravaged by starvation. They hear reports of gangs and violence in cities or neighborhoods nearby. They want to make a difference, but they're not sure they can. This journey will encourage kids and show them they can make a difference! As Christians, they can change the world by showing and telling others about Jesus and his great love for them.

Paul spent a lot of time in prison because of his faith. Depending on the size of your room, you may want to do some or all of the following things to your room to give it the feel of a prison:

● Create boulders by filling paper grocery bags with wadded-up newspaper and taping them shut. Stack and tape the paper boulders along the room walls to resemble the inside of a prison with stone walls.

● Set a pile of chains near the wall to resemble the chains that may have bound Paul.

● Tape strips of black construction paper to the walls to resemble the bars on prison windows.

● Set a fake rat in the corner of your room.

"A LIFE OF GIVING"
SERVICE RETREAT

ACTS 9-27

- Kids will learn that God is loving.
- Kids will learn to love others.

Refer to the "Retreat at a Glance" chart on page 115 to determine the gear you'll need for this journey. The chart lists supplies you'll need for each activity.

- Don't forget to select a signal!
- Have children each bring two of their favorite pizza toppings to the retreat. Have children bring ingredients they can prepare at home, such as cut-up meat or vegetables or cans of sliced olives or pineapple.
- Select an appropriate video to show the children. Look for a video that demonstrates the spirit of giving, which kids will be learning about during the retreat. If you're stuck for ideas, try *Beauty and the Least*, from Focus on the Family, or *It's a Wonderful Life*. To avoid violating copyright laws, get appropriate permission to show the video to a large group.
- You'll need to recruit male and female adult chaperons. You'll need one adult with a car for every four to six kids. Plan to meet with the adults before the retreat and explain what they'll be doing. On Friday night, they'll help with food preparation and cleanup, then sleep in the boys' or girls' sleeping area. On Saturday, they'll be driving kids to their service-project sites and helping them complete their servant evangelism projects. Before you close your meeting, be sure to thank your volunteers!
- Children will choose their service activities from the "Servant Evangelism Ideas" handout (p. 121). Collect any supplies children will use for these ideas. Write a different area of town on a slip of paper for each adult chaperon. Put this information and a photocopy of the "Servant Evangelism Ideas" handout in an envelope with the chaperon's name on it.

RETREAT AT A GLANCE

Day and Time	Activity	Supplies Required
Friday, 5:00	Arrival	Name tags, markers
Friday, 5:10	Blow Out	Various colors of bubble gum pieces (no more than five of each color)
Friday, 5:30	Pizza Assembly	Prepared pizza crusts, pizza sauce, grated mozzarella cheese, pizza pans, plates, spoons, forks, napkins, instant-drink mix, pitcher, cups
Friday, 7:00	Road to Damascus	A blindfold and feather for each child
	Paul in a Basket	Laundry baskets
	Jailed	None
	Shipwrecked	Chairs, towels, brooms, cups of water
Friday, 8:00	Break	Fruit, cookies, juice, napkins, cups
Friday, 8:30	Roll Camera	Video, VCR, television
Friday, 10:00	Devotion	"Lights Out" devotions (p. 122), Bibles
Friday, 10:30	Lights Out!	None
Saturday, 7:00	Rise and Shine	Breakfast food
Saturday, 7:45	Lunch Assembly	Lunch bags, bread, mayonnaise, mustard, knives, peanut butter, jelly, lunch meat, cheese, lettuce, plastic sandwich bags, small bags of potato chips, fruit, cookies, small surprises, juice boxes or soft drinks
Saturday, 8:30	Go in My Name	"Servant Evangelism Ideas" handouts (p. 121), envelopes, adult volunteers, other supplies as necessary (see handout)
Saturday, 12:30	Refuel	Lunches, balloons, volleyball net
Saturday, 2:00	End of Retreat	None

ROAD SIGN

● If you do this journey during the summer, it's OK to pick a night other than Friday to begin the retreat. Schedule the retreat at a time that will work for your church and your kids.

● If you can't do an overnight retreat, do a full-day meeting. Have kids arrive after breakfast and spend the morning playing the learning games and watching the video. Have kids assemble their lunches and eat them at the church, then send them out to perform their ministries of service in the afternoon. Make pizza for dinner when kids return.

● You can also do this retreat as two half-day meetings. Do the Friday-night activities one Saturday morning and have kids return the next Saturday to do their ministries.

THE JOURNEY: Friday Night

ROAD SIGN You can make name tags as simple or as complex as you want. You could provide self-adhesive name-tag stickers or set out construction paper, markers, tape, and scissors and let kids make their own.

5:00 ARRIVAL

As kids arrive, greet them and ask them to each make a name tag. Make a special effort to greet new people or friends kids might bring with them.

5:10 BLOW OUT

ROUND ROBIN
p. 7

Use your signal to get kids' attention. Explain that you'll be using it throughout the retreat. When they hear the signal, kids should stop what they're doing and focus on you for their next instructions.

Have children form a large circle. Throw the bubble gum into the circle and have children race to get a piece. After they each find a piece, have them chew the gum, blow a bubble, then get in a group with other children who have the same color of gum.

After children have formed their color groups, read the statements below, one at a time. Pause after you read each statement to allow time for kids to complete it. Have kids complete the statements in their group in a round robin style (see p. 7). Move clockwise around the circle until each child answers the question. Encourage everyone to complete the statements.

● "The best thing that happened to me this week was…"
● "The most loving thing someone else ever did for me was…"
● "The most loving thing I ever did for someone else was…"
● "The most loving thing God ever did

for me was…"

After groups have completed the last statement, say: **God has shown love to each of us in special ways. The fact that God even provides oxygen for us to breathe is a loving act from a loving God. We're going to experience God's love this weekend. In fact, we're going to be God's vehicles to show love to others. Listen to what the Bible says about that.**

Read 1 John 3:16-18. Say: **We'll be showing love to others through our actions on this retreat. We'll also be learning about a man God used to show love to others. This man's name was Paul.**

5:30 PIZZA ASSEMBLY

Set already-prepared pizza crusts at one end of a long table. Set the pizza sauce and a spoon next to the pizza crusts. Then set out grated mozzarella cheese and any toppings children have brought.

ASSEMBLY LINE
p. 7

Have children line up along both sides of the table. Then have them work as an assembly line (see p. 7) to pass the pizza crusts down the line and add sauce, cheese, and toppings. Encourage children to use different toppings to create a unique pizza each time. Once the pizzas reach the end of the line, have an adult place them in an oven and bake them. Let kids visit with each other or listen to their favorite contemporary Christian music while the pizzas are baking.

After each pizza is baked, bring it out and dig in! Serve kids beverages with their pizza. After children have finished eating, lead them in the following games.

7:00 GAMES

ROAD TO DAMASCUS

Say: **Paul had a dramatic conversion experience that helped him believe in Jesus Christ. Before Paul became a Christian, his name was Saul. Saul was on the road to Damascus when he saw a blinding light and heard a voice. The voice said, "Saul, Saul, why do you persecute me?"**

Saul fell to the ground and asked, "Who are you, Lord?" Then the voice said, "I am Jesus, whom you are persecuting."

After this experience, Saul was blind for a few days. As soon as he regained his sight, he spent every day after that serving God and telling others about Jesus. Let's see what it may have been like to be blind for those days.

Have everyone line up at one end of the room. Give kids each a blindfold and a feather. Have kids put on the blindfolds and then get on their hands and knees and try to blow their feathers to the other end of the room. Kids who successfully blow their feathers across the room can compete against each other to blow their feathers back to the starting point. Kids who didn't make it across the room with their feathers can watch.

When kids have finished blowing their feathers, have them remove their blindfolds. Congratulate all the kids for their efforts. Collect the blindfolds and the feathers. Then ask:

● **What was it like to blow your feathers across the room blindfolded?** (Hard; I couldn't tell whether I

was blowing the feather or not; it was easy if you stayed close to your feather.)

● **How was your experience with blindness just now like or unlike Paul's blindness?** (Paul didn't know if he would see again; I was glad to take off my blindfold, and Paul was glad to see again.)

Say: **Paul was glad to be able to see again after being blind. Let's find out what happened to Paul after he regained his sight.**

PAUL IN A BASKET

Say: **The Jewish leaders hated Paul. They hated Jesus, and they didn't like that Paul was always talking about Jesus. So the leaders were always out to get Paul. Once Paul had to escape from them by being placed in a basket and lowered out of a high window. Let's play a game to get a little glimpse of what that may have been like for Paul.**

Have kids help you set up an obstacle course using chairs, tables, boxes, and anything else you can find. Designate a starting line, the route kids will follow, and the finish line.

Form teams of four. Give each team a sturdy laundry basket. Have teams each place one teammate in the laundry basket and take turns racing through the obstacle course. Teams must keep their teammate in the basket at all times. Time teams as they race. The team with the fastest time wins.

Collect the laundry baskets and have kids help you clean up the obstacle course. Say: **Let's find out what else happened to Paul as he tried to tell people about Jesus.**

> **ROAD SIGN**
> Make sure kids push their laundry baskets and keep them on the floor at all times. If teams try to carry their baskets, kids could fall out and get hurt.

Jailed

Say: **Paul wasn't always able to escape from the people who hated him because he loved Jesus. He spent a lot of time in jail because of his faith. But no matter what happened to Paul, he kept believing in Jesus and showing others God's great love for them. One time, Paul was in jail with a man named Silas. While Paul's and Silas' feet were in chains and the jail doors were locked, God sent an earthquake that broke their chains and opened the doors. Paul and Silas were free. And as a result, their jailer believed in Jesus Christ. Let's see what that was like by playing a game called Jailed.**

Designate the center of the room as the jail. Choose one tagger, or "persecutor," for every 10 kids. Have the persecutors chase the children and try to tag them. When people are tagged, the persecutor can throw them in jail. When you yell "Earthquake!" children who are in jail are set free and the game starts over.

After you play the last round of Jailed, give the signal to regain kids' attention. Say: **If you think going to jail is bad, wait until you find out what happened to Paul later in his life!**

Shipwrecked

Say: **Paul often had to travel from city to city by boat to tell others about Jesus. Once his boat was shipwrecked. Let's see what a shipwreck might be like.**

Form new teams of four. Give each team a chair, a towel, a broom, and a cup of water. Tell teams they must each make a boat using all of their items. They must then move their boats from one end of the room to the other without spilling the water. Any team that doesn't use all its items or that spills water is "shipwrecked" and must sit out the rest of this game.

Observe kids as they put together their boats and move them across the room. You may need to call out "Shipwreck!" if you see water spill. After everyone is either shipwrecked or across the room, say: **You can see that Paul's life wasn't easy. We've learned how he was lowered over a wall, thrown in jail, and shipwrecked. Many other exciting and scary things happened to Paul during his lifetime. But Paul didn't mind. He was devoted to following Jesus and showing people God's love. We can follow his example and tell others about Jesus today.**

8:00 BREAK

Provide fruit, cookies, and juice for kids to snack on. Allow about 30 minutes for kids to eat their snacks, visit with their friends, and take bathroom breaks before you move on to the next activity.

8:30 ROLL CAMERA

Have children grab their pillows and meet in a carpeted area of your church. Show kids the video you've selected. Make sure at least one adult chaperon stays in the room to keep kids from bothering each other as they begin to get tired.

10:00 DEVOTION

Have the girls sleep in one area and the boys sleep in another. After children are ready for bed and tucked in, have an adult leader in each area lead the "Lights Out" devotion (p. 122).

10:30 LIGHTS OUT!

7:00 RISE AND SHINE

Start the morning with a breakfast of "energy foods." Serve foods such as oatmeal, whole-grain cereals, muffins, fruit, and juice. Avoid doughnuts or sugary cereals that might get kids wound up. Kids will need to be at their best as they serve people in your community.

After breakfast, lead kids in one or two familiar songs to start the day. Then say: **Today, we're going to show God's love to people we may never have met before. Each of you has been assigned to an adult leader. Your leader has an envelope with directions and a list of missions your group can perform. You'll meet with your leader and choose a mission. Then you'll go out and perform your mission of love in the name of Jesus. When you return, we'll meet together for lunch.**

Have groups meet with their leaders and choose a mission from the "Servant Evangelism Ideas" handout (p. 121). Have adults take kids to the supply area to collect any supplies they'll need to perform their mission. If too many groups choose the same mission and you run out of any supplies, have some groups choose different missions. After groups have col-

> **ROAD SIGN**
> Have your adult chaperons meet with you the first thing in the morning. Give each adult an envelope with directions to the area of town they'll be visiting. Show adults where they can find the supplies they'll need to carry out the ideas on the "Servant Evangelism Ideas" handout (p. 121). Assign no more than six children to each adult.

lected all their supplies, have them gather in your eating area for lunch assembly.

7:45 LUNCH ASSEMBLY

Set out lunch bags at one end of a long table. Set loaves of sliced bread at the opposite end. Set plastic sandwich bags in the center. Between the bread and the plastic sandwich bags, set out mayonnaise, mustard, peanut butter, jelly, lunch meat, cheese, lettuce, or other sandwich fixings. Don't forget to set out knives!

Between the plastic sandwich bags and the lunch bags, set out small bags of potato chips, whole pieces of fruit, and wrapped cookies.

Have kids wash their hands, then line up beside the table. Then have kids work as an assembly line (see p. 7) to make lunches for the day. They'll pass the bread down the line and create sandwiches; then they'll bag the sandwiches and put them in lunch bags with chips, fruit, and cookies.

Once the lunches reach the end of the line, have an adult place the lunches and juice boxes or soft drinks in the refrigerator. Have kids gather in the center of the room for prayer before they leave for their missions.

ASSEMBLY LINE
p. 7

> **ROAD SIGN**
> While the kids are gone this morning, have an adult place a small surprise in each lunch. Include surprise items such as candy bars, small age-appropriate toys, or a sheet of stickers. Don't tell kids about the surprises! They'll enjoy discovering them when they open their lunch bags.

8:30 GO IN MY NAME

Pray for children, asking God to show his love to people through them today. Encourage children to be bold in telling people that they are serving them in Jesus' name to show them God's love. Remind them not to accept any money for their services.

Have adults take their kids out to serve others. Remind adults that they'll need to return to the church for lunch by 12:30.

While kids are out, set up a volleyball net and blow up several balloons so kids can play Balloon Ball while they're waiting for other groups to return. Balloon Ball is played like volleyball, but it uses balloons instead of a volleyball. Kids can play with one balloon or as many balloons as they want.

PAIR SHARE

p. 6

12:30 REFUEL

When all the kids have returned, use your signal to call them to your eating area. Pass out the lunches and drinks. As kids are eating, ask for group reports about their service missions.

After kids have finished eating, have them find a partner from another service group and discuss the following questions. Pause after you ask each question to allow time for pairs to discuss it.

● **How did you feel when you found the surprise in your lunch?** (Happy; thankful; it was fun.)

● **How did people feel when you served them today?** (Grateful; surprised; they wondered why we didn't want any money.)

● **How are the feelings of the people you served like or unlike the way you felt to find your surprise?** (They were probably even more surprised; they got something for free, and we got a free surprise; they weren't sure they liked it at first.)

● **How do you think people felt when Paul showed them God's love?** (Confused because Paul used to be a bad guy; glad; grateful that Paul was willing to put himself in danger.)

● **What's been the best thing that's happened to you today?** (The smiles on people's faces when we helped them; when we washed people's cars, they offered us money even though we didn't ask for any; I met some new friends in my group.)

● **What's been the most difficult thing that's happened?** (When people made fun of us when we told them about Jesus' love; when we ran out of quarters and some people still wanted to do their laundry; it was hard work mowing lawns.)

● **What's one way you can show God's love to others this week?** (Doing the dishes for my family; telling a friend about Jesus; watching my little sister so my mom can go for a walk.)

After kids have discussed all the questions, invite them to share the things they'll do this week to show God's love. Then close with a prayer similar to this one: **Dear God, thank you for loving us. Thanks for sending Jesus to show us how to love others. Help us keep loving each other and showing your love to everyone we meet. In Jesus' name, amen.**

2:00 END OF RETREAT

Have kids play Balloon Ball again until their parents arrive to pick them up.

SERVANT EVANGELISM IDEAS

Carry out groceries for people at a grocery store.

Clean people's windshields at a mall and leave notes.

Travel with snow shovels or lawn mowers and take care of people's yards.

Clean friends' rooms.

Provide free gift-wrapping at a mall.

Deliver cups of water for anyone working outside, such as workers at a construction site or landscapers.

Take a roll of quarters to a self-service laundry facility and give them away.

Have a free carwash. Don't take any donations!

Travel the streets with rakes and rake people's yards.

Provide baby-sitting services at a mall.

LIGHTS OUT

Directions: Read the following situation, then read the Scripture passage and lead kids in discussing the questions below.

"He makes me so mad!" Kelly yelled as she slammed the door to the classroom.

"What's wrong?" Mrs. Benson asked.

"I hate my brother! Every time I turn around, he's breaking something of mine. I wish he'd never been born."

"Oh, Kelly, I don't think you really mean that, do you?" Mrs. Benson asked.

"Well, he's so mean. He calls me names and gets away with it. And sometimes he even tries to beat me up. How am I supposed to feel?" Kelly asked.

Read aloud 1 John 4:7-12. Ask:

● **What do these verses tell us about love?** (Love comes from God; God is love; we should love others.)

● **What do these verses tell Kelly about loving her brother?** (She should love him even though he's mean to her; she should tell him about Jesus so he'll understand what love really is.)

● **Is there anyone in your life who you have a hard time showing God's love to? Explain.** (My teacher, because she yells at our class a lot; my little sister, because she's always getting into my stuff; my parents, because they're always fighting.)

● **How can God help us love difficult people?** (By helping us see the good things about them; by reminding us how much Jesus loves us.)

Close in prayer and ask God to help kids love the specific people they mentioned.

Photocopy and cut out this schedule and post it where children can refer to it during the retreat. You may want to make several photocopies and post them in the areas where you'll be eating, sleeping, and playing games.

RETREAT SCHEDULE

FRIDAY

5:00	Arrival
5:10	Blow Out
5:30	Pizza Assembly
7:00	Games
8:00	Break
8:30	Roll Camera
10:00	Devotion
10:30	Lights Out

SATURDAY

7:00	Rise and Shine
7:45	Lunch Assembly
8:30	Go in My Name
12:30	Refuel
2:00	End of Retreat

TROUBLESHOOTING

Research has shown that interactive learning works. But it may be different from what you and your students are used to. If you haven't used interactive learning before, you've probably got lots of questions: How much interaction is enough? How much is too much? Will interactive learning help or hinder my success in classroom management? This section will answer some of your questions and help you maximize your classroom management while you're maximizing kids' potential for learning.

Begin by setting a few simple classroom rules with kids. To generate your rules, use the following basic categories:

- Respect for God.
- Respect for others.

Use a cross chart (see p. 8) to help children discuss what each of these categories should look and sound like in your classroom. For example, kids may say respect for God sounds like no bad words or being reverent when people are praying. They may say respect for others looks like kids keeping their hands to themselves or not interrupting each other. When you finish the cross charts, post them in your room to remind kids of the rules they've helped create.

Brainstorm with your class to determine consequences for violating your classroom rules. If kids have trouble coming up with consequences themselves, suggest a verbal warning for the first rule violation, a timeout for the second violation, and a report to a parent for the third violation. Once you've established consequences together, it will be your job to kindly but firmly enforce them.

Make your class a positive place by affirming kids when they follow the rules. When you see kids showing respect for God or others during class, point it out. Other kids will soon try to catch your attention by following a good example. If you catch and "expose" kids who are following the rules, you won't catch many kids who are breaking them.

The following chart lists some common classroom management problems that may arise with interactive learning. While this table isn't exhaustive, it can help you avoid some of the pitfalls of interactive learning and make the most of this innovative teaching style. Simply look for the problem you're experiencing in the left-hand column. Then check out the possible solutions in the right-hand column.

PROBLEM	POSSIBLE SOLUTIONS
Kids won't participate fully in groups.	**1.** Look at your room arrangement. Are the tables and chairs easily moved in circles? Or are they set up in rows like a traditional classroom? Your room arrangement can help or hinder interactive learning. Make it easy for kids to work together by placing chairs in circles before class. **2.** If a few children seem to dominate discussion, give groups small, colored tokens to monitor each person's input. (You can make colored cards from construction paper or use colored blocks or Lego pieces.) For example, in a group of four, give one child five red tokens, another child five yellow tokens, the third child five black tokens, and the fourth child five blue tokens. Each time a child speaks, he or she must set a token in the center of the group. When a child is out of tokens, he or she cannot speak again. Tell groups their discussions aren't finished until they've used up all their tokens.
Kids always come to me for the answers.	**1.** The first time a group comes to you for help, refer them to another group. Say something like "I think group A could help you with that. Why don't you go ask them?" Resist the temptation to be the information center of the classroom. Kids will learn more if they have to struggle with a problem. They'll also boost their self-esteem when they're able to succeed without your rescuing them. **2.** If other groups aren't able to help, go ahead and offer your assistance to kids. Begin by asking kids to suggest solutions.

I can't get kids' attention when they're working.	Use the signal (see p. 6). You may need to remind kids how the signal is supposed to work. They won't automatically know; they need training.
The signal doesn't work in my class.	If you use the signal and children still don't respond, try asking for a five-point response. Say something like "When I use the signal, I expect five points of response. I'm looking for listening ears, eyes forward, hands still, feet still, and body facing toward me." Point out specific children who violate the five-point response. You might say, "Kelly, feet still please," or "Bryan, eyes forward. Thank you."
My class is too loud.	If you think the class is too loud, first determine whether you're hearing good noise or bad noise. Good noise is the hubbub of children learning. Because kids are excited, their voices may be getting louder. If you're hearing too much good noise, remind kids to show respect for others by speaking softly so everyone can learn. Bad noise is the sound of children who are distracted. They're off task and causing disruptions to class learning. If you're hearing too much bad noise, remind kids of your classroom rules and their consequences. Carry out your discipline plan if necessary.
There's always one child who won't participate.	Use the buddy system. Pair the reticent child with a child who is likely to draw him or her out. Have the partners work on the task at hand. Tell them they must work together to succeed.

Kids won't stay on task.	**1.** Use the role assignments from page 7. Remind the taskmaster that it's his or her job to keep the group on task so they can do all the fun things you've planned. **2.** Ask for reports after group time. If children know you'll hold them accountable, they'll work even harder to get the job done.
No matter what I do, the same child is disruptive.	Use a "cool-down chair." Have the disruptive child sit in the cool-down chair until he or she feels ready to rejoin the group. If you use this discipline method, don't lose sight of why you're using it. Your goal *is not* to humiliate the child; your goal *is* to help the child calm down. Consider putting books, puzzles, or stuffed animals in the corner so children can wind down and relax. Let the child tell you when he or she is ready to rejoin the class—but don't be afraid to use the cool-down chair again if you disagree with the child's assessment.
I have a lot of bright students in my class. Won't they be held back if they're placed in groups with slower students?	Encourage bright students to help slower students in their groups succeed. Bright students may actually learn even more if they're placed in a situation where they have to teach what they know. You may need to remind them that their groups' success depends on everyone's participation.